Gateways to Westward Expansion

Using Literature and Primary Sources to Enhance Reading Instruction and Historical Understanding

Ann Claunch and Linda L. Tripp

Teacher Ideas Press

An imprint of Libraries Unlimited

Westport, Connecticut • London

Library of Congress Cataloging-in-Publication Data

Claunch, Ann.
    Gateways to westward expansion : using literature and primary
sources to enhance reading instruction and historical
understanding / Ann Claunch and Linda L. Tripp.
        p. cm.
    Includes bibliographical references and index.
    ISBN 978–1–59158–748–4 (alk. paper)
    1. United States—Territorial expansion—Study and teaching (Secondary)   2 United States—
Territorial expansion—Sources.   3. West (U.S.)—History—Study and teaching (Secondary)
4. West (U.S.)—History—Sources.   5. Historical fiction, American—Study and teaching (Secondary)
6. Historical fiction, American—Sources.   7. Literacy—Study and teaching (Secondary)
I. Tripp, Linda L.   II. Title.
    E179.5.C49   2009
    978'.02—dc22   2008056123

British Library Cataloguing in Publication Data is available.

Library of Congress Catalog Card Number: 2008056123
ISBN: 978–1–59158–748–4

First published in 2009

Libraries Unlimited/Teacher Ideas Press, 88 Post Road West, Westport, CT 06881
A Member of the Greenwood Publishing Group, Inc.
www.lu.com / www.teacherideaspress.com

Printed in the United States of America

The paper used in this book complies with the
Permanent Paper Standard issued by the National
Information Standards Organization (Z39.48–1984).

10 9 8 7 6 5 4 3 2 1

Contents

CHAPTER 10—

THE WOMEN OF THE WESTWARD MOVEMENT 105

Introduction

Understanding history is essential for American democracy. A healthy circulatory system of active, informed citizenry keeps our nation vibrant. A deep awareness of the people and events of history is central to being an educated citizen. This knowledge is the perspective against which events of today are considered and judged.

As teachers of students and teachers of teachers, we are well aware of the pressures that both face on a daily basis. History is often pushed to the background in the nation's curriculum landscape as the testing climate emphasizes skills. To prevent a painful demise of our democracy, our students need desperately to learn the content of history. To teachers of social studies, developing these essential understandings is paramount. But often, our students *do not* have the necessary literacy skills on which they will be tested and which allow them to deal with the content they need. Teachers are caught in the middle. Do they teach history content even when student skills are inadequate to the task, or do they devote precious time and resources to the development of sorely needed literacy skills?

This is a false choice. These goals are not incompatible or mutually exclusive. Our book, ***Gateways to Westward Expansion,*** was developed to aid teachers in planning lessons that simultaneously address content and literacy skills. It is possible to engage student thinking in important content in ways that develop and promote critical reading and writing. For students, we introduce history through fiction then expand the students' knowledge through primary sources and exemplary nonfiction books, or we may build historical understanding through primary sources then incorporate quality literature to develop skills and interest.

Gateways moves chronologically through the westward expansion period of history, beginning with the Lewis and Clark Corps of Discovery in 1805 and progressing into the twentieth century with the orphan trains and the role of women in the development of the West. Each of the 10 chapters presents historically significant events while emphasizing individuals or groups that made a difference in history. These individuals and groups represent a variety of both mainstream and lesser known voices: peoples impacted by the westward expansion of the United States.

Teachers may pick and choose from a variety of activities and strategies that address basic content, develop historical context, incorporate literature, build literacy skills, and engage students in historical thinking. Each strategy, though linked to specific content, has broader applications to many different contexts and allows teachers to develop a cumulative repertoire for teaching and linking history and literacy.

The Components of Each Chapter

Chapter Preview

At the beginning of each chapter, we have included a list of the featured books, primary source documents, and teaching strategies addressed in the chapter. This list provides teachers with an easy-to-access reference for planning and for finding information on particular strategies and books.

Gateway Books

Our primary purpose is to engage students in the narrative of our past through well-written fictional accounts of history. Although we do not believe that fiction exclusively can or should teach history, we do believe that it provides a doorway to unofficial historical research for even the most reluctant learner. Just as the adult watches the movie or reads the book *Braveheart* and begins to wonder about William Wallace (Was he a real person? Did he really stand against the British at York?), so, too, does a fictional representation of events and characters, such as Sacagawea, a buffalo soldier, a young Native American forced into an Indian school far from home, or an orphan train rider, prompt students to want to know more.

Fictional books offer other dimensions as well. Well-written historical fiction can evoke the emotions of an event in a way that a textbook or even good non-fiction does not. Furthermore, these books allow students to enter into the perspective of characters involved in history, often offering viewpoints not always considered in the mainstream.

Therefore we begin each chapter with a selection of reviewed, quality historical fiction and non-fiction that illuminates the chapter content. Our selections include novels and picture books for older readers that can provide the hook that engages interest and the emotional connection that sustains inquiry. Fiction allows students to see themselves in history, to encounter multiple perspectives, and ultimately, to understand that history is not just a dry, dull series of events, but is really the story of people—their choices and decisions, and the consequences of those choices. Teachers may choose these books as read-alouds, novel study selections, or for students' independent reading.

Historical Background

Each chapter topic is developed in a narrative reflecting the most current thinking and research around the event or era. This information is secondary source content providing basic information about the historical event or time period featured in the chapter. It summarizes material around important people, places, and happenings. This page may serve as quick and easy-to-digest content for the teacher or may be reproduced and used with students as an assigned or guided reading.

Primary Source Documents

Each chapter features one or more reproducible primary source documents to be used with students in developing historical context for the time period. The documents take students from the broad view of the topic offered in the historical background into a very specific piece of content. Use of the primary source documents to delve more deeply into a topic engages students as historians and researchers of history, teaching vital thinking skills in the process.

Strategies to Teach History

Each chapter offers at least one method for teaching history through the primary source documents, with specific suggestions to help students look closely, think deeply, make inferences, and draw conclusions from the material before them.

Strategies to Teach Reading

Literacy skills of reading and writing are fostered in each unit through use of the featured literature or the reproducible Historical Background. The strategies focus on such vital components of critical reading as fluency, comprehension, vocabulary development, summarizing, and so forth. Though the suggested activities are tied to the specific chapter content, the strategies can be replicated with other content selections. Both the history strategies and the reading strategies are cumulative so that with each chapter, the teacher builds a repertoire of teaching possibilities.

Graphic Organizers

One or more graphic organizers that support the strategies described are available in the chapter. The graphic organizers are designed to help the teacher quickly and efficiently prepare for instruction. However, research also suggests that the use of graphic organizers assists students in organizing their thinking, understanding content, and retaining information.

Unit Timeline

At the end of each chapter, we have included a teaching timeline as a suggested organizer for teachers in planning and implementing the unit activities. The timeline was designed to suggest a possible order to the activities that will help students make connections and move from broad ideas to more specific, in-depth study. The timeline is a suggestion only; teachers should feel free to eliminate or order activities according to the needs of their classrooms.

Bibliographies

In addition to the featured Gateway Books, we punctuate each chapter with more extensive bibliographies that include student selections of fiction and non-fiction that support further study and adult selections for teachers who wish to deepen their own knowledge. Where appropriate, we add lists of additional primary source documents and web-sites that might be helpful to teachers in planning the unit.

Assessment

Regular and on-going assessment is a vital part of the teaching and learning process. The best assessments accomplish several objectives. The first objective is to keep teachers in touch with what students truly understand about the material they are covering and where gaps in their understanding or misconceptions occur. The teacher can then adjust his teaching as needed. A second but no less important goal of assessment is to inform students of their own progress. A third objective, required by all school systems, is to give grades and inform parents of student progress.

Short answer and multiple choice tests have a place in assessment and grading as they can provide a quick snapshot of student mastery of content information. However, when the goals of learning are deeper understanding and critical thinking, more complex assessment measures are needed. Performance assessments as defined by Marzano and others are multi-step projects that allow for a variety of pathways through which students can demonstrate levels of mastery and understanding.

It is not the goal of this book to provide a complete assessment package because we believe these are best designed by the teacher in the context of her classroom and with knowledge of her particular group of students. However, most of the history strategies and reading strategies outlined in these chapters lend themselves to performance assessment tasks. To this end, we have included a separate list in Appendix A of possible performance tasks, along with a generic rubric outline in Appendix B, which can be adapted for various tasks. We suggest, however, that an activity not be given to students as an independent task for assessment unless they have had previous experience with the protocol.

Conclusion

In conclusion, all these components are intended to give the teacher options. Each chapter can stand alone as a mini-unit, which may be explored in depth or covered briefly, depending on the time available. Teachers may choose one, two, or all components in any given chapter and may include one, more, or many of the chapters in their overall study of westward expansion. It is our hope that these options support good teaching and learning opportunities and provide teachers with tools for efficient planning and teaching.

CHAPTER 1

The Lewis and Clark Expedition

Chapter Preview

- **Gateway Books:** *Sacagawea* by Lise Erdrich; *New Found Land* by Allan Wolf
- **History Strategies:** Now/Then Comparison; Using Primary Source Documents
- **Reading Strategy:** Found Poetry
- **Historical Background:** On the Road with the Corps of Discovery
- **Primary Source Document:** Shoshone Robe
- **Graphic Organizer:** Lewis and Clark Supply List

Gateway Books

Erdrich, Lise. 2003. *Sacagawea.* Minneapolis, MN: Carolrhoda Books.

Immortalized by statues and commemorative coins, the young Native American woman who accompanied Lewis and Clark across a continent carrying her baby on her back has become a legendary figure of almost mythical proportions. Sacagawea herself left no written record of her journey; we know her through the words of Meriwether Lewis and William Clark, as recorded in their extensive journals.

In writing about Sacagawea, Lise Erdrich has remained true to the tenets of historical biography. She does not invent conversations or suggest how Sacagawea thought or felt about various incidents and encounters. She tells the story simply, in prose that evokes the early-eighteenth-century wilderness and native life. Where the historical record is incomplete, Erdrich says so and, in the afterword and author's notes, shares interpretations commonly held by historians.

Who was Sacagawea? She was a captive, perhaps a slave, a young wife, a teenage mother, a knowledgeable forager, an interpreter, a sister, and a friend. Though she may have pointed out landmarks as the Corps of Discovery neared Shoshone territory, she did not literally guide Lewis and Clark across the continent. She did, however, make significant contributions to the expedition with her knowledge and calm demeanor.

Sacagawea remains a powerful role model of a young woman of courage and fortitude. The book by Lise Erdrich, enhanced by the beautiful illustrations of Julie Buffalohead, offers students the opportunity to reach back through the years to meet this young woman of mystery and legend.

Wolf, Allan. 2004. *New found land.* Cambridge, MA: Candlewick Press.

The author uses prose and poetry in this young adult novel to tell the story of the Lewis and Clark expedition as it might have been experienced by various members of the Corps of Discovery. At nearly 500 pages, the book is deceptively long, but easy to read, as different characters, including Lewis, Clark, Sacagawea, Pierre Cruzette, George Drouillard, the Fields, and others—even Seaman, the dog—recount the hardships and adventures of the trail in free verse format. Based on and faithful to the historical record, the author imagines the feelings and emotions that must have accompanied the experiences of the journey.

Strategies to Teach History

Using primary sources in the classroom transports students into the past. Students will physically lean forward at their desks as artifacts, images, and texts are read from different time periods. Allowing students to work with primary sources essentially allows the students to touch the past through their senses: they see tools, they hear the words from a text, they smell black gun powder from a long ago battle. But to use primary sources effectively in the classroom requires more than bringing interesting items into the class. The study of primary sources requires a careful curriculum orchestration to build the historical story and the historical context around the sources to achieve historical understanding.

Sacagawea, by Erdrich, a picture book, provides a gateway into a deeper study of the Native Americans during the early nineteenth century. The study adds an additional challenge by calling into question how we study an indigenous people when all written texts are authored by those outside the culture.

Now/Then Comparison

To understand the world of Sacagawea, a foundational activity for the young historian is to draw a distinction between past and present. Being able to compare life as we know it and life as it was lived in the past starts with helping students to think outside the present. Here is an opportunity to combine a study of primary sources with a **Now/Then** comparison.

Beginning with what students know, ask students to brainstorm as a class the supplies needed for a six-month camping trip. As students offer suggestions, the teacher records the ideas in a central location. Students and teachers then group the recorded supplies into broader categories, for example, shelter, clothing, and cooking.

The teacher then introduces the Lewis and Clark supply list (**Graphic Organizer**) and repeats the categorization activity. Placing the lists side by side, challenge students to determine what supplies are the same and why, and what supplies are different and why. Nudging students toward the sharp distinction between the world of Lewis and Clark and the present will help build historical context.

Using Primary Source Documents

When analyzing primary sources with young students, we like to encourage teachers to structure the lessons by using images as an introduction to primary sources and by scaffolding the analysis into three levels: the aesthetic, the historical interrogation, and the written analysis. Using images is an inclusive strategy for all students. Students who are unseasoned readers or who are learning English as a second language can fully participate while analyzing images.

STEP 1

On completion of an oral reading of *Sacagawea,* ask students to list as a class what they have learned about Sacagawea. The purposes of this preliminary list are to begin a discussion, to distinguish fact from fiction, and to learn how to check sources. The class-generated list is then sub-divided into two categories: "What We Think Is True" and "What We Question about Sacagawea." This list will serve as an anchor point throughout the study of Sacagawea as we revisit and verify knowledge about Sacagawea or the Shoshone or delete information identified as myth.

STEP 2

Now we are ready to look at the first primary source. Break students into small groups and examine the picture of the Shoshone robe.

First Level (Aesthetic)

Ask the groups to respond to the image of the Shoshone robe subjectively. Prompt students by asking the following questions:

1. What do you see?
2. How does the image make you feel?
3. What is the image and what is its use?

Second Level (Historical Interrogation)

The teacher leads a formal guided discussion. Students are arranged so that they may look at a projected image of the Shoshone robe on the screen as well as a smaller reproduction provided to their group. Pose the following questions:

1. Who created this object?
2. What was the object's use? How do you know?
3. Who took the picture?
4. Why was this picture taken?

Third Level (Written Analysis)

Ask students to form pairs and complete a chart using the following questions. This level forces a close, guided look at the image. Students notice and identify aspects of the image that were overlooked in the other two levels.

1. List all the objects you see in the image.
2. What activities do the images depict?
3. Based on what you have observed, list three things you might infer from the photograph.

4. What questions do you have about the Shoshone people during the early nineteenth century?
5. Where could you find answers?

The three levels of image analysis are important to complete. Each requires the students to think in a different way and to discover new information about historical images.

Strategies to Teach Reading
Found Poetry

Old Life

A young girl

Gathered roots and berries

Where three rivers flowed

Captured and carried away

Amidst noise and confusion

Further and further from all that she knew.

New Life

Earth lodge village like upside down bowls

She sang to the corn to help it grow

Chased hungry birds from the grain

Carried home harvest in a bull boat

No more than sixteen

Given in marriage

A young girl

Sacagawea

These lines comprise a found poem using words and phrases from the first pages of Lise Erdrich's ***Sacagawea.*** Found poems offer an alternative format for capturing critical information and exploring vocabulary. Marzano et al. (2001), in ***Classroom Instruction***

That Works, identify summarizing as the ability to extract critical information and as 1 of 10 strategies that positively and significantly affect student achievement.

To create a found poem, students begin by gleaning words and phrases from the text to capture essential ideas and information. Having students work with partners or in triads can enrich the experience as they discuss and negotiate with one another to choose the *most* important words and phrases. It is also helpful if the teacher suggests a minimum and maximum number, based on the amount of text under consideration. Having a limit within which to work forces students to consider choices. Marzano defines the necessary steps in summarizing as deciding what information to keep, what to eliminate, and what to substitute—exactly the process of creating found poetry.

Once selections are made, students arrange the words in phrases to form a poem. They may add words, if necessary, to complete an image or idea or to provide a transition. A title completes the poem and emphasizes the main idea.

Teaching Activity

Using the text of **Sacagawea** by Lise Erdrich for found poetry helps students to consider Sacagawea as a person and her importance to the Corps of Discovery. Begin by reading the entire text aloud to the group, then model the process of found poetry with the first few pages. Use an overhead from a page or two of the text or have a student copy the text portion on a large sheet of paper so that the whole class can see. The teacher can think aloud as he/she highlights words and phrases, explaining why each is being considered. Choose many words or phrases, then model the process of elimination, engaging students in a discussion of which phrases best capture the significant event or events in Sacagawea's life. Note that the found poem at the beginning of this section may serve as a model for students, but teachers will need to demonstrate the process.

Student Activity

Once a found poem has been modeled from beginning to end, students are ready to try the process on their own. Divide the text of **Sacagawea** into manageable sections (a page or two) and give each group of students a section with which to work. Provide the following directions:

1. Read your section of the text carefully several times. Group members may take turns reading aloud so that everyone has an opportunity to both see and hear the words.
2. Highlight (if text has been reproduced) or copy (if students are working from the book) words and short phrases that best capture the events or emotions of the text.
3. As a group, narrow your selections to the required number. Discuss your reasons for including some choices and eliminating others.
4. Arrange your chosen words and phrases in poem format. Decide on a title for your poem.
5. Copy your poem on the poster provided. Illustrate it if there is time.

Display

The resulting poems can be posted around the room on a time line capturing the life of this interesting person. Students may need to do some research to attach approximate years to the various sections of Sacagawea's life. Selected pages or characters from *New Found Land* by Allan Wolf may be used in the same way.

Unit Timeline

We recommend the following order of activities to maximize the connectedness of the unit. Teachers may rearrange or eliminate activities to suit the needs of their students and the purposes they have for the material.

- Share the book *Sacagawea* by Lise Erdrich as a read-aloud with the entire class.
- Present students with historical background information from "On the Road with the Corps of Discovery" (**Historical Background**). This could be an independent reading assignment, a shared reading (see chapter 4) with the class, or a lecture summary by the teacher, to be determined by the age and ability of the students.
- Use the **Now/Then Comparison** from **Strategies to Teach History** with the Lewis and Clark supply list (**Graphic Organizer**). List student conclusions on a piece of chart paper.
- Use the **Found Poetry** suggestions in **Strategies to Teach Reading** to develop and support reading skills and to help students look more deeply into information about Sacagawea.
- Provide a conclusion to the **Found Poetry** activity by completing the "What We Think Is True" and "What We Question about Sacagawea" charts suggested in **Strategies to Teach History.**
- Use the "Shoshone Robe" **Primary Source Document,** as suggested in **Strategies to Teach History,** to look more deeply at Shoshone life and culture. Compare conclusions to what was learned from the study of Sacagawea.
- Read further using selections from the bibliographies, add to the information charts, and compare to information in available textbooks. Return periodically to the "What We Think Is True" and "What We Question about Sacagawea" charts. Lead students to add new information and understandings, correct misconceptions, and generate new questions.
- Organize independent research for students on various topics suggested by study. This will allow students to go deeper into various areas of interest and add to the class store of knowledge. Note that teachers may want to reserve independent study activities until later in the study of westward expansion, when students can choose from a greater variety of people, places, events, and times in history. This will also minimize the demand for duplicate copies of secondary sources.

Adult Bibliography

Ambrose, Stephen. 1997. *Undaunted courage.* New York: Simon and Schuster.

This work represents a complete and stirring account of the Corps of Discovery by a noted historian.

Brandt, Anthony. 2002. *The journals of Lewis and Clark.* Washington, DC: National Geographic Society.

Brandt offers an abridged version of the journals, updating spelling and punctuation and eliminating repetition to make the journals accessible to the reader. Periodic summaries provide context and fill in gaps left by the journals or by the authors' decision to eliminate some material.

Student Bibliography

Blumberg, Rhoda. 2004. *York's adventures with Lewis and Clark: An African American's part in the great expedition.* New York: HarperCollins.

York, a slave who was William Clark's body servant, was the only African American associated with the Corps of Discovery and was a great curiosity to the Native Americans. The book details York's part in the expedition and reveals the limited facts that are known of his life before and after.

Bruchac, Joseph. 2000. *Sacajawea.* New York: Scholastic Signature.

The alternating voices of Sacagawea and Capt. Clark relate the major events of the expedition to Pomp, Sacagawea's son.

Edwards, Judith, and Sally Wern Comport. 2003. *The great expedition of Lewis and Clark: By Private Reuben Field, member of the Corps of Discovery*. New York: Farrar, Strauss, Giroux.

A fictional account, based on historical record, of the expedition told in the folksy style of a young Kentucky farmer who accompanied Lewis and Clark.

Patent, Dorothy. 2002. *The Lewis and Clark trail: Then and now.* New York: Penguin.

Dorothy Patent has captured the route that Lewis and Clark took from St. Louis to the Pacific and, through text, paintings, and photographs, contrasts the changes that have taken place two centuries later.

————. 2003. *Plants on the trail with Lewis and Clark.* New York: Clarion Books.

This book and its companion—*Animals on the trail with Lewis and Clark*—highlight the scientific aspects of the expedition.

Smith, Roland. 1999. *The captain's dog.* New York: Gulliver Books.

This book provides another study in viewpoints. Seaman (Capt. Lewis's dog) is the narrator of the events of the expedition.

On the Road with the Corps of Discovery

If you traveled in Idaho, Oregon, Washington, or Montana, would you expect to see woolly mammoths, unicorns, seven-foot-tall beavers, erupting volcanoes, or blue-eyed Indians speaking Welsh? In 1803, Thomas Jefferson was the newly elected president of a new country. The majority of the population calling themselves Americans lived east of the Mississippi, and these were the curiosities that even intelligent and educated men like Jefferson expected to find in the unexplored territories west of the Mississippi.

In January, 1803, Congress funded an expedition to explore the area from the Mississippi River to the Pacific. Jefferson hoped for a water route connecting the eastern half of the continent to the Pacific to provide for direct trade with the Orient and to establish an American presence in areas under British, French, or Spanish influence. The Louisiana Purchase of 1803 changed the mission from exploration of foreign territory to gathering information about an expanded America. Jefferson envisioned a peaceful voyage of geographic, cultural, and scientific discovery. He charged his secretary, Capt. Meriwether Lewis,

The object of your mission is to . . . discover the most direct and practicable water route across this continent. . . . Along the way you should also endeavor to make yourself acquainted with the names and nature of any Indian nations you encounter. . . . Treat them in the most friendly and conciliatory manner.

Lewis enlisted his friend, William Clark, as his co-captain, and together they selected a cadre of men, who became known as the Corps of Discovery. In May 1804, Lewis and Clark and their men embarked from St. Charles on the Missouri River using a 55-foot keelboat and two canoe-like pirogues. The Corps wintered at the mouth of the Knife River near the Hidatsa and Mandan villages. Here they accepted the services of a French trapper named Touissant Charbonneau, probably for the language skills of his Shoshone-speaking wife, Sacagawea. In February 1805, Sacagawea gave birth to a son, and on April 7, the party of two captains, 29 men, one woman, one infant, and one dog departed from the winter camp en route to the Pacific.

Over the ensuing months, the expedition members sailed, rowed, poled, pulled, and portaged the two pirogues and six smaller dugout canoes over 2,000 miles of unmapped territory. Fourteen miles represented a good day's progress. They faced storms, floods, animal stampedes, and starvation. In December 1805, they built winter quarters near present-day Astoria, Oregon, and traveled to the coast for a glimpse of the Pacific and the wonder of a beached whale carcass.

When winter snows melted the following spring, the return journey began. Lewis and Clark reached St. Louis on September 23, 1806, marking the last day of the Corps of Discovery. Remarkably, the Corps suffered only one death on the long and treacherous journey.

The Corps of Discovery provided carefully documented, first-hand information about the vast regions of the continent west of the Mississippi, including detailed drawings and descriptions of 178 previously unknown plants and 122 "new" animals, along with maps of the physical terrain. This information helped to open the west to Euro-American entry.

In addition, the Corps established significant contact between the population of the east and nearly 50 tribes of the West and Northwest, from the farming communities of Hidatsa and Mandan to nomadic hunting groups such as the Teton and Yankton Sioux. The expedition was peaceful in intent and, generally, in execution, but it continued an ideology in which the Native Americans were considered children and government was cast as the "great white father," a pattern of thinking that would persist into the next century.

Shoshone Robe

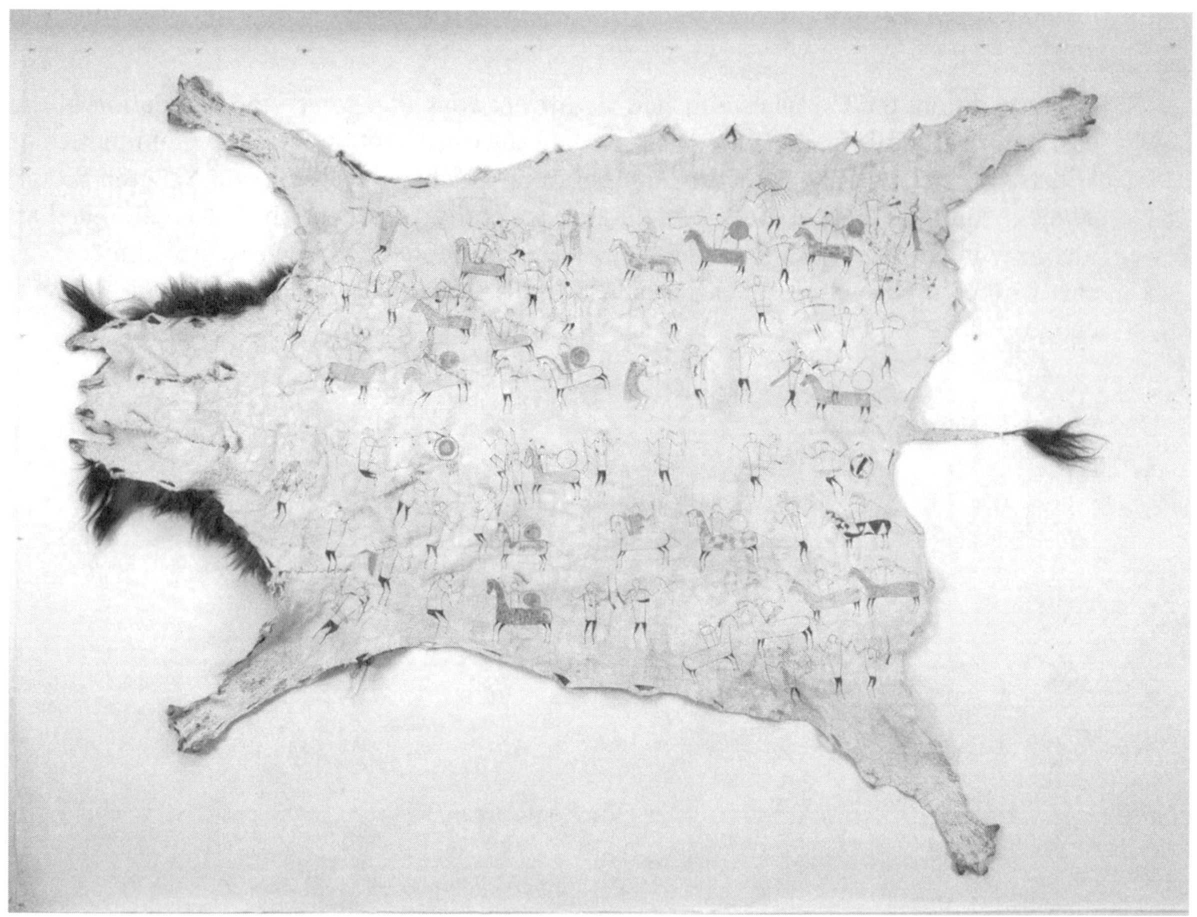

Courtesy of Monticello/Thomas Jefferson Foundation, Inc.

From *Gateways to Westward Expansion: Using Literature and Primary Sources to Enhance Reading Instruction and Historical Understanding* by Ann Claunch and Linda L. Tripp. Westport, CT: Teacher Ideas Press. Copyright © 2009.

Lewis and Clark Supply List

Now	Then
	Hand compass
	Telescope
	Thermometer
	Sextant
	150 yards of oiled cloth
	30 steels
	Handsaws
	Hatchets
	Whetstones
	Iron corn mill
	Tablespoons
	Mosquito curtains
	Fishing hooks and lines
	Soap
	3 bushels of salt
	Writing paper, ink
	12 dozen pocket mirrors
	144 small scissors
	Ivory combs
	Silk ribbons
	Vermillion face paint
	Coats
	Frocks
	Shoes
	Woolen pants
	Blankets
	Knapsacks
	Lancets
	Syringes
	Tourniquets
	Physic pills
	Maps
	Dictionary

1. What on your list is the same as on the Corps of Discovery's list? What is different?
2. What items on Lewis and Clark's list are unfamiliar to you? What might they be for? How could you find out?

CHAPTER 2

The Santa Fe Trail

Chapter Preview

- **Gateway Book:** *Along the Santa Fe Trail* by Ginger Wadsworth
- **History Strategy:** Windows into the Past
- **Reading Strategy:** Pre-reading and Post-reading Vocabulary
- **Historical Background:** The Santa Fe Trail
- **Primary Source Document:** Painting, *Arrival of the Caravan at Santa Fe*
- **Graphic Organizer:** Pre-reading and Post-reading: Vocabulary Study

Gateway Book

Wadsworth, Ginger. 1993. *Along the Santa Fe Trail: Marion Russell's own story.* Morton Grove, IL: Albert Whitman.

Sunrise and sunset, thunderstorms and howling coyotes, tales of gold and Indians, buffalo trails and wallows, wagon caravans and circles, games of leapfrog and dare base, gathering buffalo chips and calling tarantulas, birth and death—Marion Russell's remembrances paint a picture, at once dramatic and mundane, of life on the Santa Fe Trail in 1852. Marion was seven years old when she, her mother, and her brother traveled the trail for the first time with the intention of settling in California. She was in her eighties when she told her stories to her daughter-in-law. Winnie Russell recorded the stories as Marion told them, and Marion read and corrected the writing. Those stories were published as *Land of Enchantment: Memoirs of Marion Russell along the Santa Fe Trail.* In 1993, Ginger Wadsworth adapted Marion Russell's text for young people as *Along the Santa Fe Trail: Marion Russell's Own Story.*

Because Wadsworth maintains Marion's own words, the text has the intimate feel of sitting with Marion and listening to her tales. The reader is transported to the early 1850s and can experience the trepidation and wonder of that long caravan of "white-hooded" wagons, loaded with merchandise and swaying behind the tired, sweaty, straining mules. On reaching Santa Fe, Marion's mother discovered that the money and jewels meant to finance the rest of the journey had disappeared, forcing the family to settle in Albuquerque. Though disappointed that their dream of California is lost, the family—and their readers—realize that they have lived the adventure of a lifetime. Wadsworth comments in a pretext note that Marion's words "reflect the perspective of the white settler," although Marion does wonder, in portions of her memoirs not included in this text, about the Native Americans "who watched with bitter eyes that vast migration."

Strategies to Teach History
Windows into the Past: Rationale

The concept of the passage of time is difficult for the young historian to grasp. The study of history asks students to conceptualize an unfamiliar world and the mores of a distant society. To really understand the Santa Fe Trail, students need to build a mental image of what it was like to travel during the mid-nineteenth century, how people dressed, what they ate, and the day-to-day challenges they faced. To accomplish the mental construction of a past world, students need many visual images and overt discussions of likenesses and differences between the present and the past.

Windows into the Past is an assignment that combines the study of historical time with the development of research skills by exploring the social and cultural aspects of a different period. Studying elements that are familiar to students, such as food and fashion, helps students scaffold an understanding by comparing and contrasting the past to the present.

The basis of this assignment is exploring the *cultural universals* (Brophy and Alleman, 2005). Cultural universals are elements that all cultures share (food, fashion, architecture, transportation, entertainment, and tools/technologies). The cultural universals are human needs and social experiences that are found in all societies, past and present. Gathering different images and artifacts promotes the study of elements that are the same and those that are distinctively different.

Windows into the Past: Teaching Activity

Historical images help students build a mental picture of the past. Reading historical images is a unique skill and needs guided practice. The first activity is done in a whole-class setting to provide modeling of the process.

The materials needed are images of *Arrival of the Caravan at Santa Fe* for every two students (copied onto 8.5 × 11-inch sheets of paper) and a projection of the same image large enough for everyone to see. Use the following questions to elicit student descriptions of the cultural universals on the Santa Fe Trail:

1. What are the modes of transportation present in the painting?
2. What was the fashion of the day? Did everyone dress alike? Were there differences in socioeconomic status?
3. What are the different types of tools needed on the Santa Fe Trail?
4. Do you see any evidence of entertainment?
5. According to the image, what was cooking like on the trail?
6. What did people use for shelter on the trail?

Windows into the Past: Student Activity

With an introduction to the cultural universals, students are now ready to explore more independently and with more depth. Divide students into small groups of four or five. Ask each group to select (or the teacher may assign) a cultural universal to research for the years of the Santa Fe Trail (1820–1880). The teacher may wish to assist students in finding suitable books, web-sites, videos, and other resources. Note that useful resources and web-sites are included in the bibliography section of this chapter.

Directions to the students are as follows:

1. Study your selected universal for the assigned era. Infer, based on your research, why various forms of the universal were popular during that particular time period.
2. Plan a creative display and oral presentation of what you have learned from your study of the universal for the class.
3. All presentations must be accompanied by visuals and be interactive.
4. Research resources must be present.

Sharing

After students have presented **Windows into the Past** to their classmates, display the exhibits in your classroom or in the school library in a history gallery. Invite other classes to visit the gallery. Provide a notebook and encourage visitors to comment on what they learned from viewing the **Windows** displays.

Strategies to Teach Reading

Vocabulary in Reading

Vocabulary development is an essential part of reading comprehension. Students who can read words but do not know what they mean will be hampered in understanding text. Sometimes this is a matter of nuance, particularly in historical contexts. A student reading a text on early-nineteenth-century sailing may recognize the word *ship,* but his internal visualization, based on experience, may be of a modern-day freighter, rather than a sailing vessel (Claunch 2002). Teachers need to maintain awareness of the vocabulary demands of the texts students read.

Choosing Words for Instruction

Isabel Beck et al. (2002) suggest that teachers organize words into three tiers. In the first or bottom tier are words in everyday usage such as *mother, baby, dinner.* These are words for which students will not need instruction. In the third or top tier are esoteric words specific to a particular text but unlikely to be encountered by students outside of that context such as *permafrost.* These words may need a brief explanation, but their low utility does not warrant extended instruction. Beck suggests that words targeted for instruction come from the middle tier of words. These are words with which students may be unfamiliar but which are likely to be encountered on a recurring basis. Of course, a word's location in a specific tier is not fixed, but will differ depending on the age and background knowledge of the students. Words from ***Along the Santa Fe Trail*** that are potential candidates include *dread, astir, wallow, forage,* and *perilously.*

Teaching Activity

Pre-reading and post-reading is a vocabulary strategy that has the benefit of expanding and enlarging vocabulary and developing the skill of using context to determine meaning while assisting students in attending to the particular nuances of the text they are reading.

In advance of the lesson, the teacher selects some key words from the story and prepares a simple, five-column graphic organizer (see the **Graphic Organizer**). The columns are headed as follows: Word; Page Number; Pre-reading Definition; Text Sentence; Post-reading Definition. The teacher can fill in the first two columns in advance of reproducing the **Graphic Organizer** or may provide the information for students to complete the columns at the start of the lesson. The third column is to be completed by students as a pre-reading activity, in which they use prior knowledge to make a best guess as to what the selected words mean. If they have no knowledge of the word, they can write "don't know." The pre-reading work can be done individually or in groups with as much or as little discussion as the teacher wishes. The teacher may scaffold students by guiding discussion to encourage connections to other words and to past experiences and by discouraging the "don't know" response, except as a last resort. The teacher may wish to set limits on the use of "don't know."

After completion of the first three columns, the book is read. This may be a read-aloud by the teacher or may be independent reading by students, depending on their skills and the number of copies available. The fourth and fifth columns are a post-reading activity. In column 4, the students record the text sentence in which the word occurs. In column 5, they write their new definition of the word based on the reading of the story and the context in which the word is placed. Again, this may be an individual, partner, small-group, or whole-group activity. The teacher has the option of providing as much scaffolding as she thinks necessary for the group or for individuals through discussion and sharing.

The key to the success of this strategy is the selection of words. The words should be within the students' *zone of proximal development* (Vygotsky 1962)—words that are likely to be unknown but not unknowable. This means that the definition, once known, should be within the capacity of the students to understand. The teacher must also determine that there is adequate context in the story for students to develop meaning for the selected words.

Instructions to Students

1. Consider each word your teacher has selected for study. Use what you know about how the word sounds, how it looks, and how it is like other words you know to make a guess about its meaning.
2. As you or someone else reads the story, listen for sentences containing each word you are studying. Your teacher has given you a page number clue.
3. After the story is read, record the sentences containing each selected word in the correct column on your paper.

4. Consider the sentence and the story as a whole to write what you now think the word means. You may have an entirely new definition or you may find you were correct or partially correct in your first definition.
5. Discuss what you have learned about the word meanings with your teacher and classmates.

Sharing

Opportunities for follow-up discussion are critical. Students should be encouraged to share ways in which they linked words to prior knowledge and how the context of the story helped them determine or modify meanings. Struggling students and second-language learners will especially profit from this modeling.

Unit Timeline

- The **Windows into the Past** activity described in **Strategies to Teach History** is a powerful beginning for any unit as it places students in the correct historical context for the remainder of the information they will encounter. Share the **Primary Source Document** *Arrival of the Caravan at Santa Fe* as described as a basis for a cultural universals discussion. Depending on time available, students may do an in-depth study of several cultural universals, including transportation, shelter, tools, clothing, food, and entertainment. If time is very limited, the teacher may choose to focus on fewer, such as transportation as a background for the Santa Fe Trail, continually reminding students of differences in other factors as well.
- Introduce the **Pre-reading/Post-reading Vocabulary** activity from **Strategies to Teach Reading** using words pre-selected by the teacher. Have students complete the first three columns.
- Share the book *Along the Santa Fe Trail* by Wadsworth. This may be done as a read-aloud or in small groups. Discuss the experiences of Marion Russell and her family on the trail. Relate these experiences to the **Windows into the Past** activity.
- Complete the vocabulary activity by filling in remaining columns of the **Graphic Organizer.** Discuss the meaning of the words and whether they are still in use today. If so, has the meaning changed?
- Read the **Historical Background** reproducible. This may be done in a whole group, in a small group, or assigned as independent reading.
- You may wish to do a map activity tracing the route of the Santa Fe Trail.
- If desired, organize students for independent research and study.

Adult Bibliography

Bacon, Melvin, and Daniel Belgin. 1972. ***Bent's Fort: Crossroads of cultures on the Santa Fe Trail.*** Palmer Lake, CO: Filter Press.*

A chronology of the trail beginning with the initial journey by Becknell. This is an excellent overview of the trail, from its inception to its closing with the advent of the railroad.

Dary, David. 2000. ***The Santa Fe Trail: Its history, legends and lore.*** New York: Alfred A. Knopf.

Extensive research and powerful storytelling place the people and experiences of the Santa Fe Trail in the broader historical context of the development of the Southwest, particularly Santa Fe and New Mexico.

Drumm, Stella M., ed. 1982. ***The diary of Susan Magoffin, 1846–1847: Down the Santa Fe Trail and into Mexico.*** New Haven, CT: Yale University Press.*

A young wife, following her husband, chronicles the journey of a pioneer merchant from St. Louis to Bent's Fort, through Santa Fe and down into Mexico in the mid-nineteenth century. The story is layered with observations of the landscape, the interactions and clashes between cultures, and the fear and intrigue of the impending war with Mexico. Although the diary has been criticized as a newlywed woman's romanticized view of the world (she refers to her husband as *mi amor,* "my love" in Spanish), the descriptive nature of the diary informs the reader about the hardships of travel and the interactions of multiple cultures.

Gregg, Josiah. 2001. ***Commerce of the prairie.*** Santa Barbara, CA: Narrative Press.

Credited as one of the definitive journals of the westward movement, Josiah Gregg vicariously takes readers into buffalo hunts, gold mining, and Mexican agriculture. He also describes in loving detail "an opposing array of death-dealing savages." The rich narrative style of Josiah Gregg influenced Susan Magoffin when she penned her diary 14 years later.

Student Bibliography

Carson, William C. 2002. ***Peter becomes a trail man.*** Albuquerque: University of New Mexico.

The language is flowery and evocative of the writing of an earlier era as it details the adventures of young Peter, who is traveling with a wagon train to Santa Fe in search of his father. The book accurately reflects daily life on the trail and many of the attitudes and ideas of Euro-Americans of that time. The teacher may want to mediate the roles and depictions of Native Americans in the book.

Lavender, David. 1995. ***The Santa Fe Trail.*** New York: Holiday House.*

A clearly written text tracing the history of the Santa Fe Trail from its inception in 1821 to its demise in 1879. The author provides insights into the importance of the trail in history, including why it came into being and its impact on people and places. Most appropriate for eighth grade and up, teachers of elementary students may pre-select smaller segments of the text for use.

McDonald, Megan. 2003. ***All the stars in the sky.*** New York: Scholastic.

Young Florrie Mack Ryder keeps a diary of her life on the Santa Fe Trail with her mother, brother, and step-father, a wagon-master. The book, which can be read by elementary students, parallels the Marion Russell memoir in many ways and gives flesh and human dimension to day-to-day life on the trail.

Tripp, Valerie, and Jean-Paul Tibbles. 1998. *Josefina saves the day.* Middleton, WI: Pleasant.

One of the books of the American Girl series, this volume takes place in 1820s Santa Fe as Josefina plans to trade with the American wagon train arriving in the plaza. This book, which will appeal to students who need easier material to read, considers the Santa Fe Trail trade from the point of view of the local Hispanic population. Other books in the Josefina series provide a context for life in the Mexican territories at that time.

Note: An asterisk marks those books particularly useful for the **Windows into the Past** activity in the **Strategies to Teach History** section.

Web-sites

While working with the **Windows into the Past** assignment, students can access images and texts to enhance their study at the following web-sites:

Gilder Lehrman, http://www.gilderlehrman.org/
Library of Congress, http://www.loc.gov/
National Archives and Records Administration, http://www.archives.gov/
Our Documents, http://www.ourdocuments.gov/

The Santa Fe Trail

The Santa Fe Trail initially began in Franklin, Missouri, and ended in Santa Fe, New Mexico. Throughout the nineteenth century, the trail head changed with the needs of the merchants and with natural disasters. In 1829 a flood destroyed Franklin, and the gateway to the trail became Arrowrock, Missouri. Later history books identify Booneville, Missouri, as the starting place for the Santa Fe Trail. Here merchants could load their westbound wagons with merchandise shipped to that point by steamboats.

The Santa Fe Trail was primarily a commercial enterprise, begun for the purpose of selling goods to the Mexican territories. In 1821 Mexico had recently won her independence from Spain. Under Spanish rule, trade with the United States was illegal. Economic interchanges were done in secrecy. With Mexican independence, the trade restrictions were lifted. The first traders carried goods on mule back across the trail, but early in 1821, Missourian William Becknell organized a small group of farmers to take the first wagons west to Santa Fe. This involved risk as no one was sure how a party of Americans would be received. However, the Becknell group was actually guided to Santa Fe by five Mexican soldiers whom they met along the trail. Mexico encouraged their continued trade, and the Santa Fe Trail blossomed into a flourishing economic venture between the two countries.

The route itself was 775 miles long, running over the Cimarron cutoff and crossing five present-day states: Missouri, Kansas, Oklahoma, Colorado, and New Mexico. Becknell's undertaking in bringing furniture, face powder, dry goods, and hardware to Santa Fe was profitable, and others followed in his footsteps. There was a reverse trail as well: returning wagons and Mexican traders brought Mexican silver, wool, and mules back to the United States. Although the first endeavors used pack mules, the huge Conestoga wagons soon became the standard conveyance along the trail.

The trail flourished for over 60 years, until the completion of the railroad in 1880 made wagon travel obsolete. During the years of its existence, the character of the trail changed. The Mexican-American War of 1846–1848 made the trail important as a military supply route. Several forts were established during this time. After hostilities ceased, the trail resumed its trade function but increasingly became a route to the West. Among the many travelers were stagecoach passengers, gold seekers, fur trappers, and adventurers as well as the traders.

The commerce of the trail created points of contact between cultures. Traders enjoyed the flamboyant fandangos in Santa Fe, which brought together people of all ages, sexes, and walks of life. Returning to the United States, they brought an appreciation for aspects of the Spanish/Mexican culture, artifacts, and language. The native populations along the trail were initially friendly, but over time, tensions with the Plains Indians increased as pressure was put on their homelands and hunting grounds by constant traffic and increasing settlement. Frustrations mounted and attacks on the wagon trains became more frequent. The forts became increasingly important, and a significant military presence was established along the trail to protect the emigrants.

From its inception, the Santa Fe Trail was primarily a man's world. The goal of the traders was to haul goods to New Mexico and back for a profit but to maintain their homes and families in the United States. Few women traveled the trail, but in 1829, as a bride, 18-year-old Susan Shelby Magoffin accompanied her husband to Santa Fe and into the Mexican territories. The journal that she kept along the trail documents that journey and gives insights into the day-to-day operation of a wagon train. Later, a few families joined the wagon trains for protection on their way to California. Marion Russell, her mother, and her brother traveled the trail in 1852, and her remembrances of trail life offer another picture of the time and place.

Painting, *Arrival of the Caravan at Santa Fe*

Copy of original lithograph ca. 1844. Courtesy of the Palace of the Governors (MNM/DCA). Negative #045011.

From *Gateways to Westward Expansion: Using Literature and Primary Sources to Enhance Reading Instruction and Historical Understanding* by Ann Claunch and Linda L. Tripp. Westport, CT: Teacher Ideas Press. Copyright © 2009.

Pre-reading and Post-reading: Vocabulary Study

Word	Page Number	Definition	Text Sentence	Post-reading Definition

From *Gateways to Westward Expansion: Using Literature and Primary Sources to Enhance Reading Instruction and Historical Understanding* by Ann Claunch and Linda L. Tripp. Westport, CT: Teacher Ideas Press. Copyright © 2009.

CHAPTER 3

The Alamo

Chapter Preview

- **Gateway Books:** *Voices of the Alamo* by Sherry Garland; *Inside the Alamo* by Jim Murphy
- **History Strategy:** Differing Perspectives
- **Reading Strategy:** Readers' Theater
- **Historical Background:** The Alamo
- **Primary Source Document:** Quotes from Santa Anna and Stephen Austin
- **Graphic Organizer:** Weighing the Evidence

Gateway Books

Garland, Sherry. 2000. *Voices of the Alamo.* New York: Scholastic Press.

Sherry Garland's gentle prose transports us through the centuries at the site now known as the Alamo. A Payaya Indian, friars, Texians, Tejanos, and soldiers are among the historical figures and ordinary people who appear to briefly share their viewpoints against the backdrop of the mission whose name became a rallying cry for courage and freedom. This book is an experience in time travel that reminds us that history belongs as much to the individuals whose names are never recorded or remembered as it does to those whose names echo through the ages.

The history of the Alamo is succinctly traced in this book, which provides a counterpoint and complement to more in-depth historical accounts such as Murphy's book, described next.

Murphy, Jim. 2003. *Inside the Alamo.* New York: Delacorte Press.

The Alamo occupies a unique place in U.S. history. For the average American, it stands as one of the most widely known and least understood of historical encounters and symbolizes fighting for freedom against overwhelming odds.

Murphy's very readable book traces the development of events from February 23, 1836, when Santa Anna's army arrived in San Antonio de Bexar, to March 6, 1836, when that army captured the Alamo and annihilated its defenders.

Emotionally charged historical events sometimes receive biased retelling. Murphy presents a balanced treatment of the Alamo conflict and its leading players—flawed individuals exhibiting greatness in extraordinary circumstances. Through this book, we better understand the issues as they were perceived by both sides. The central text of the book is faithful to the narrative of events, but many insets (from small text boxes to double-page spreads) provide biographical information and insights into the lives of the people involved as well as the legendary events such as the line in the sand.

Strategies to Teach History

Differing Perspectives

In 1835, Americans in the Texas territory began a rebellion against Mexican control. One of the most remembered battles of the Texas Revolution is the battle of the Alamo. Following are excerpts from two speeches (see the **Primary Source Document**). The first speech was given by Santa Anna, who viewed the Americans living in Texas as "lawless foreigners." The second excerpt is from Stephen Austin's Texas Independence Address, in which he calls the Americans living in Texas "an oppressed people."

The honor of the nation being interested in this engagement against the **bold and lawless foreigners** who are opposing us, His Excellency expects that every man will do his duty, and exert himself to give a day of glory to the country, and of gratification to the Supreme Government, who will know how to reward the distinguished deeds of the brave soldiers of this Army of Operations. (Antonio Lopez de Santa Anna, 1836, Alamo attack order)

When a people consider themselves **compelled by circumstances or by oppression,** to appeal to arms and resort to their natural rights, they necessarily submit their cause to the great tribunal of public opinion. The people of Texas, confident in the justice of their cause, fearlessly and cheerfully appeal to this tribunal. In doing this the first step is to show, as I trust I shall be able to do by a succinct statement of facts, that our cause is just, and is the cause of light and liberty—the same holy cause for which our forefathers fought and bled—the same that has an advocate in the bosom of every freeman, no matter in what country, or by what people it may be contended for. (Stephen F. Austin, 1836, Texas Independence Address)

Who was right? When students encounter two opposing views, it is important to weigh the evidence. This takes research and requires students to consider both points of view.

Differing Perspectives: Activity

STEP 1

Students read the quotes carefully. The teacher records questions that students brainstorm about the province of Texas. The teacher should encourage students to think about *Inside the Alamo* and other readings done by the class as they create the questions to be posted. The purpose of these questions is to explore different points of view and serve as a catalyst for student research. Examples of questions based on the reading of the speech excerpts and the **Gateway Books** *Inside the Alamo* and *Voices of the Alamo* appear below. Encourage students to use both **Gateway Books** as resources to explore different perspectives:

- Who owned Texas?
- What was the advantage of being a Texian versus the advantage of being an American?
- Why did Santa Anna think he had the right to fight against the defenders of the Alamo?
- If Texas was a part of Mexico, what gave Texians the right to revolt?

Note: Texian was the spelling for Anglo-Americans living in the Texas territory. Texan became the spelling after statehood.

STEP 2

Multiple copies of *Inside the Alamo* are required for the next activity. Check with the school library as several copies may be held within the school district. Public libraries are also very helpful and will collect copies of books from different branches for teachers. Divide the class into small groups of four and provide each group with a copy of *Inside the Alamo* and the **Graphic Organizer** for this chapter, "Weighing the Evidence." Students are then instructed to read through the following biographical sketches intermittently placed throughout the book. Group members take turns reading the sketches aloud.

> Stephen Austin, p. 11
> Santa Anna, p. 28
> Jim Bowie, p. 35
> David Crockett, p. 38
> William Barrett Travis, p. 41
> James Fannin, p. 54
> Juan Seguin, p. 61
> Jose de la Pena, p. 67

STEP 3

Using "Weighing the Evidence," the **Graphic Organizer,** students are asked to re-read the biographical sketches and the primary source excerpts to determine evidence for one of two statements posed by the teacher. Some groups should be assigned the first statement and other groups the second:

1. Americans have the right to revolt.
2. Mexicans have the right to attack.

As student groups read, they gather evidence and record on the **Graphic Organizer** information to support or refute either the right to revolt or the right to attack. On completion of the chart, students then compose a statement about the ownership of the Texas territory that can be supported by the evidence collected.

STEP 4

Groups with opposing viewpoints prepare and participate in a debate with the rest of the class as audience. At the end of each debate, the audience is encouraged to ask the debate teams questions. Debate guidelines can be accessed on the web. After students have heard all the evidence, assign them to do a quick-write opinion paper regarding ownership of the Texas territory, either by rights or by settlement. Emphasize that their thinking must be supported by evidence. This paper is an excellent assessment of historical understanding.

Strategies to Teach Reading

Readers' Theater

Voices of the Alamo offers a perfect opportunity for students to develop fluency skills through the medium of *readers' theater.* Readers' theater differs from traditional drama in that performers read from, rather than memorize, their texts. Props and staging are also minimal or nonexistent, so the process is easily implemented and can be accommodated in a variety of settings.

Kuhn (2005) suggests that teaching fluency follow these general guidelines:

1. Teacher reads the material aloud to model fluent reading.
2. Group discussion and related activities are used to address comprehension.
3. Repeated rereading by students is scheduled.

Readers' theater provides a purpose for students to engage in the repeated rereading necessary to develop fluency.

PREPARATION

A technique that can be used to scaffold less fluent readers involves preparing the text to show phrasing. A single slash represents a pause, and a double slash stands for a longer stop.

I am/a Payaya maiden,/

gathering pecans/beside the river.//

When flowers/blanket these hills in spring/

and buffalo thunder/across the plains,/

my heart sings/ with joy.//

Preparation of the text can be done in advance by the teacher to demonstrate phrasing for the students. For better readers, it is a useful exercise to have students mark their own texts with slashes to show meaning chunks. This encourages students to think about meaning and how it is expressed through oral reading.

ACTIVITY

Sixteen voices are represented in ***Voices of the Alamo,*** one on each two-page spread. Each voice can be assigned to individual students or to teams of two. Teaming is one scaffold that can support less fluent readers. After hearing an oral model and determining the meaning and pronunciation of unknown words, students should practice reading the material several times: independently, to a partner, or to a small group. The final performance can be as informal or sophisticated as desired, though performance for an audience is an essential element in making this a real reading experience for students.

Unit Timeline

- Garland's ***Voices of the Alamo*** provides a succinct overview of the history and importance of the Alamo and is therefore an excellent beginning point. A teacher read-aloud of this picture book appropriate for older readers can be followed by a discussion of events leading up to the battle as well as the various viewpoints represented.
- The overview provided by ***Voices of the Alamo*** should be followed by a more in-depth look at the history involved. The **Historical Background** provided for this chapter can be reproduced for students to read independently, in small groups, or as a class.
- Students who have done the **Windows into the Past** study of cultural universals suggested in chapter 2 ("The Santa Fe Trail") will have a background for the time period in which the battle of the Alamo took place. Teachers may wish to briefly review this information with the students.
- The "Weighing the Evidence" (see the **Graphic Organizer**) activity using Murphy's book ***Inside the Alamo*** (described in **Strategies to Teach History**) will promote deeper historical understanding as students consider the differing perspectives surrounding the battle of the Alamo and the Mexican-American War.
- Developing and presenting a readers' theater on ***Voices of the Alamo,*** as described in **Strategies to Teach Reading,** provides an excellent culminating activity for this unit. It brings the study of the Alamo full circle and allows students to practice fluent reading in a meaningful way.

Adult Bibliography

Davis, William C. 1998. ***Three roads to the Alamo: The lives and fortunes of David Crockett, James Bowie, and William Barret Travis.*** New York: Harper Perennial.

Three Roads to the Alamo provides a look at a historical event from three different perspectives. Davis parallels our **Gateway Book** for young adults by providing an unbiased look at the Alamo and the causes leading to the conflict.

Lemon, Mark. 2008. ***The illustrated Alamo, 1836.*** College Station, TX: State House Press.

What did the Alamo look like before, during, and after the battle? ***The Illustrated Alamo*** allows the reader, through an array of historic images, to step into the past and imagine what Bowie, Crockett, and Travers saw as they faced their final hours.

Nofi, Albert. 2001. *The Alamo and the Texas War of Independence: September 30, 1835 to April 21, 1836.* Cambridge, MA: DaCapo Press.

Situating the battle of the Alamo within the historical context of the Texas War for Independence provides the reader simultaneously with a panoramic view of the conflict and a microscopic view of several battles.

Student Bibliography

Fisher, Leonard E. 1987. *The Alamo.* New York: Holiday House.

This older book by a well-known nonfiction author provides the historical background of the Southwest that explains the conflict between Texas and Mexico. Primary documents are embedded in the text.

Garland, Sherry. 1998. *A line in the sand: The Alamo diary of Lucinda Lawrence.* New York: Scholastic.
———. 2001. *In the shadow of the Alamo.* San Diego, CA: Harcourt (Gulliver Books).

These two books by one of our featured authors present differing perspectives on the battle of the Alamo. The main characters represent, respectively, the daughter of Texian settlers in Gonzales, Texas, and a 15-year-old boy from a small Mexican village conscripted into Santa Anna's army. Their collective experiences bring reality and poignancy to the events and emotions surrounding the battle.

Sullivan, G. 1997. *Alamo!* New York: Scholastic.

The author frames his account by noting that individual perspectives on events at the Alamo may be different for Anglo-Americans, Hispanic Americans, and Native Americans. He traces the history of the settlement of the Texas territory and the relationships that led to and proceeded from the battle of the Alamo.

The Alamo

In 1836 a small band of Texian (Anglo-American) and Tejano (Texans of Mexican descent) settlers withstood a siege of 10 days at the Mission of San Antonio de Valero, better known as the Alamo. Although they were ultimately defeated, the phrase "Remember the Alamo" became the rallying cry for Texan independence, and the Alamo stands today as a shrine to bravery and courage in the face of overwhelming odds.

The mission which would become that rallying point was built in 1718 by Spanish missionaries, who intended to convert the local Native Americans to Christianity and thereby produce willing laborers for the Spanish landowners. The process was less than successful, and the complex of buildings that became known as the Alamo fell into disrepair. By the time of the siege, great chunks of the wall were missing, and the chapel roof had caved in, leaving mounds of debris in the interior.

Tensions between the United States and Mexico developed as early as 1821, when Anglo-Americans led by Moses and Stephen Austin began settling in the Texas territory. Initially, the Mexican government encouraged settlement by foreigners with the provisions that they become Mexican citizens and that slavery be prohibited. Many of the early settlers, including the Austins, swore allegiance to the Mexican government and intended to live in peaceful cooperation. However, lured by the promise of inexpensive land, the Anglo population swelled to 16,000 by 1830. Concerns developed on both sides: the Mexican government had issues with Anglo-Americans' nonpayment of taxes and disregard of the slavery prohibition, and the settlers grew increasingly worried about their lack of representation in the government and about unilateral decisions made in Mexico City concerning the territory.

In 1833 Santa Anna seized power and the government became decidedly anti-American. The settlers in the Texas territory rebelled. The first battle of the Texas War of Independence took place at Gonzales, Texas, on October 2, 1835. By December, Mexican rule had been eliminated in the territory. Within weeks, Santa Anna had amassed an army of 6,000, many of them conscripted. The untrained and inexperienced Mexican army, followed by 1,500 *soldaderas* (wives, girlfriends, family), endured a brutal forced winter march through inhospitable mountains and deserts without adequate food and water. Many died. The army did not arrive in San Antonio in one body, but straggled in over days and weeks.

The 189 men (plus women and children) who took refuge in the Alamo from Santa Anna's advancing army believed they were fighting for freedom. Once the siege was enjoined, they had little choice. Santa Anna had an overwhelming advantage, and he refused to negotiate. Surrender meant almost certain death. The only option was to fight until defeated.

From February 23 to March 5, 1836, the defenders defied Santa Anna behind the crumbling mission walls. The small band of freedom fighters included both Texians and Tejanos. Command of the fort was in the hands of 26-year-old William Barret Travis. Jim Bowie, for a short time co-commander, was gravely ill and bedridden. The best known defender was David Crockett, a frontiersman and former congressman from Tennessee.

From *Gateways to Westward Expansion: Using Literature and Primary Sources to Enhance Reading Instruction and Historical Understanding* by Ann Claunch and Linda L. Tripp. Westport, CT: Teacher Ideas Press. Copyright © 2009.

Travis repeatedly sent letters declaring his intention to defy surrender and pleading for reinforcements from the American government. None came. On March 6, Santa Anna ordered an all-out assault. The walls were breached and the defenders killed to a man. In April, the Texan army, under General Sam Houston, defeated Santa Anna at San Jacinto, gaining independence for Texas. The rallying cry for the Texas troops was "Remember the Alamo!"

Quotes from Santa Anna and Stephen Austin

Excerpt: Speech Made to Santa Anna to His Men before Attacking the Alamo

The honor of the nation being interested in this engagement against the bold and lawless foreigners who are opposing us, His Excellency expects that every man will do his duty, and exert himself to give a day of glory to the country, and of gratification to the Supreme Government, who will know how to reward the distinguished deeds of the brave soldiers of the Army of Operations.

—Antonio López de Santa Anna, Alamo attack order (1836)

Excerpt: Stephen Austin from the Texas Independence Speech

When a people consider themselves compelled by circumstances or by oppression, to appeal to arms and resort to their natural rights, they necessarily submit their cause to the great tribunal of public opinion. The people of Texas, confident in the justice of their cause, fearlessly and cheerfully appeal to this tribunal. In doing this the first step is to show, as I trust I shall be able to do by a succinct statement of facts, that our cause is just, and is the cause of light and liberty—the same holy cause for which our forefathers fought and bled—the same that has an advocate in the bosom of every freeman, no matter in what country, or by what people it may be contended for.

—Stephen F. Austin, Texas independence address (1836)

Weighing the Evidence

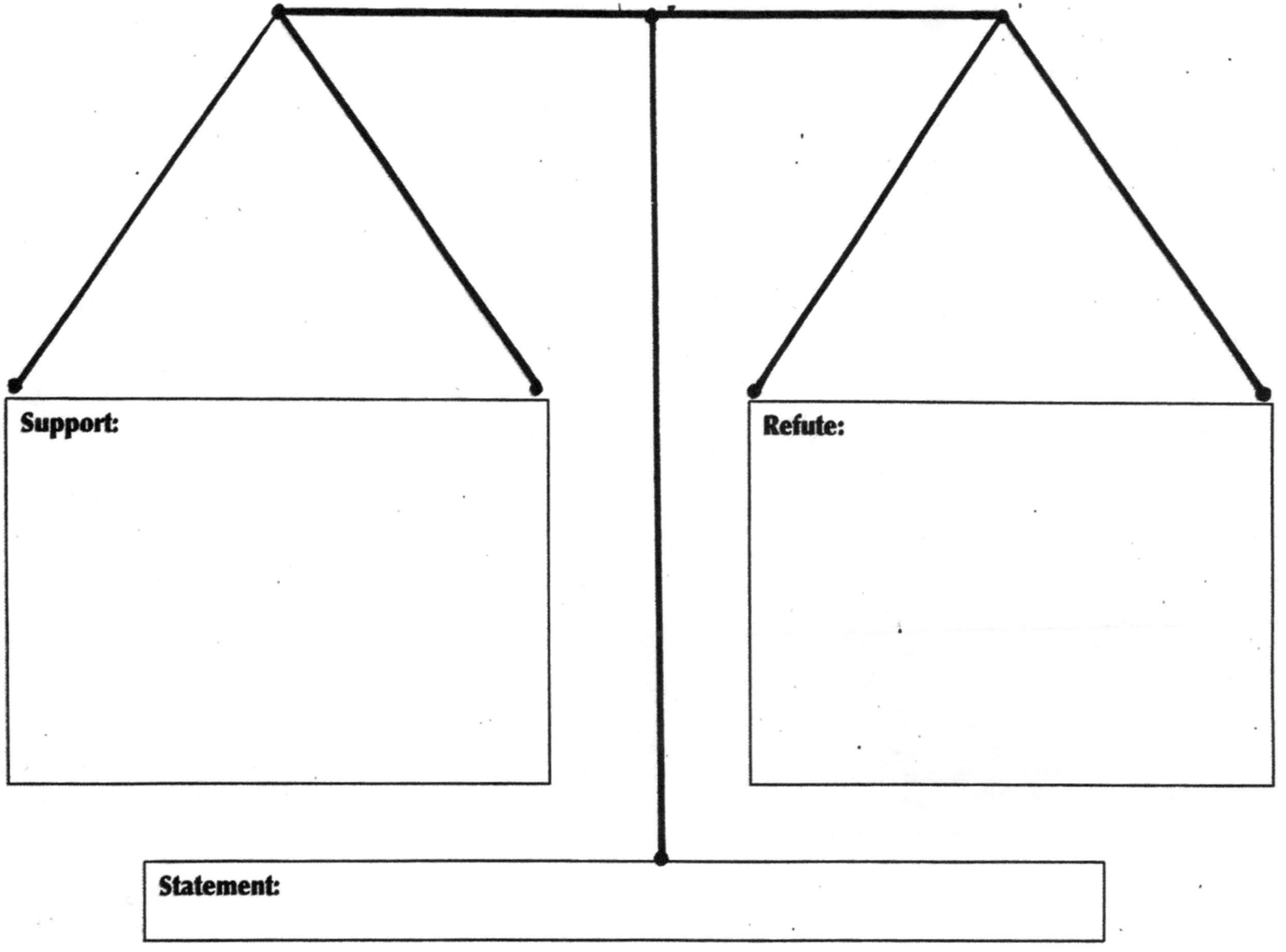

From *Gateways to Westward Expansion: Using Literature and Primary Sources to Enhance Reading Instruction and Historical Understanding* by Ann Claunch and Linda L. Tripp. Westport, CT: Teacher Ideas Press. Copyright © 2009.

CHAPTER 4

The Oregon Trail

Chapter Preview

- **Gateway Books:** *Seeing the Elephant* by Joyce B. Hunsaker; *Words West* by Ginger Wadsworth; *A Heart for Any Fate* by Linda Crew
- **History Strategy:** Studying the Individual in History
- **Reading Strategy:** Shared Reading for Older Students
- **Historical Background:** The Overland Trail
- **Primary Source Documents:** Image of Ezra Meeker
- **Graphic Organizer:** Pre-writing Biographical Sketch

Gateway Books

Hunsaker, Joyce B. 2003. *Seeing the elephant: Voices from the Oregon Trail.* Lubbock: Texas Tech University Press.

In the 1800s, the phrase "seeing the elephant" referred to the journey west to California and Oregon. Travelers did not expect to see a literal elephant; instead, the great beast symbolized both the exotic adventure and deadly perils of the trail. Travelers often likened the storms, stampedes, disease, and accidents common to trail life with having seen the "tracks of the elephant."

Nine individuals, including Narcissa Whitman, Jesse Applegate, Ezra Meeker, and Catherine Sager, who traveled the Overland Trail between 1836 and 1878, are profiled in this featured selection. Hunsaker seamlessly weaves their own words, drawn from actual diaries and journals, together with factual information from established sources to develop a first-person narrative for each individual that documents his or her experience, perspective, and investment in the great migration. Each chapter is carefully footnoted and followed by interpretative comment.

The author notes that these voices reflect the dominant Anglo-Saxon Christian culture of the time as these were the individuals who left written records. However, through summaries, discussion points, and questions based on primary sources, at the end of each chapter, the author leads the reader to consider the perspectives of less visible participants: African Americans, Hispanics, Native Americans, and Asians. A 54-page student workbook and teaching guide is available from the publisher's web-site (http://www.ttup.ttu.edu).

Seeing the Elephant, as reading material, is most appropriate for high school students, but the activities and discussion points are adaptable for middle school, and even for elementary school.

Wadsworth, Ginger. 2003. ***Words west: Voices of young pioneers.*** New York: Clarion Books.

Wadsworth's book is organized differently and is more accessible to a younger audience. Chapters address topics related to trail life such as preparations, chores, accidents, and entertainment. Historical information is interspersed with quotes and stories from varying young people who traveled the westward trail. Many of the individuals profiled in ***Seeing the Elephant*** are quoted in this book also.

The perspectives offered are not as broad as in ***Seeing the Elephant;*** however, the book explores various reasons that individuals and families traveled west to Oregon, California, and other destinations. The travelers' actual words bring life and individuality to this great migration.

The book is well illustrated with maps, photographs, paintings, and reproductions of primary documents. There are numerous half-page and full-page insets giving more detailed information on the places, people, and artifacts of everyday life on the trail. The book is appropriate for students from upper elementary through high school.

Crew, Linda. 2005. ***A heart for any fate.*** Portland: Oregon Historical Society Press.

Seventeen-year-old Lovisa King, along with her parents, brothers and sisters, and nieces and nephews, traveled the Oregon Trail in 1845. Historical records indicate the names of family members who left Missouri and of those who arrived in Oregon, but no one in this large, extended family kept a written record of the journey. Crew therefore felt free to imagine the journey itself, which she does in vivid, carefully researched detail. Our engagement with her likeable characters makes us a part of the journey from its joyous, festive beginnings, with nightly dances, a picnic atmosphere, and buffalo hunts, to tediousness, accidents, worsening conditions, exhaustion, sickness, starvation, and death.

This novel for young adult readers brings to life the immensity of the task undertaken by these early emigrants, their courage, resourcefulness, prejudices, and mistakes, and the life lessons learned along the way. The book is illustrated with photographs and concludes with information about the lives of the survivors at the end of the trail.

Strategies to Teach History

Studying the Individual in History

People make history. Students may not remember the exact dates of historical events, but they will remember the individual or collective stories of a group of individuals who made history. Challenging students to think past the date or the historical event and delve into the study of the individuals (in this case, those who traversed the Oregon Trail) transforms the study of history from simplistic memorization into a complex, multi-layered story with varied outcomes. The decisions and the routes followed by individual travelers in search of gold, land, or adventure ignited a change in our national story.

When studying the individual in history, we want students to ask questions: Who were the travelers of the Oregon Trail? What was the motivation for taking such a high-risk journey for uncertain outcomes? What new technology made the Oregon Trail possible at this particular time in history? What obstacles had to be overcome? What types of occupations made the journey possible at all? Surveyors, cartographers, and guides are not often immediately associated with the Oregon Trail but played an integral part.

Through the stories of individuals, important values, such as courage in the face of great opposition, striking out in a new direction, selflessness in helping others, ingenuity in founding or building an institution, or leadership in a cooperative effort to achieve a common goal, are revealed. What inner strengths did the pioneers possess to persevere against the unknown, lack of food and water, extreme weather conditions, violence from other travelers, or fear of Indian raids? All these questions lead to a greater understanding of the historical context of the Oregon Trail.

EXPLORATORY LEVEL

To begin a study of historical figures, the teacher can structure the research in three levels. The first level is the *exploratory level*. At this level, students read widely with the purpose of discovering all the different types of people and names associated with the Oregon Trail. Students are assigned, over a week period, to develop a list of five people and their connection to the Oregon Trail. Students collect the names of individuals and their contributions (using the graphic organizer) by reading about the Oregon Trail in the library and on the Internet. While the students are reading independently, the teacher is bringing resources and reading excerpts at the beginning of class. ***Words West,*** one of our featured books, introduces students to many different individuals and brings the larger picture of the Oregon Trail into focus for students.

At the end of the week, students share the collected names with one another in small groups or in a large group with the purpose of introducing to the class a variety of interesting individuals and their connections to the trail. The teacher may record all the names on a list for students to review. After sharing, each student or small group selects one person to research further.

COLLECTION LEVEL

Students move into the second level of research, the *collection level*. At this level, students are still reading widely but are now focused on one person. Each student or small group searches for all information available about the selected person: biographies, images, diaries. At this point, students become biographers and begin asking questions about their chosen individual.

Biographers begin with basic questions to set the stage of the individual's life. As the research progresses, questions unique to the individual represented will emerge. Following are examples of some basic questions with which students can begin:

- Where was the person born?
- Who were his parents?
- Did the person have siblings?
- What was his/her childhood like?
- At what age did he/she travel the Oregon Trail?

- What were the significant events in this person's life?
- What was the motivation for this person to travel the trail?

Through the process of asking questions, students develop a time line of the person's life and of all the people who are associated with the selected individual. Research time can be expanded or limited, depending on the teacher's unit timeline. Students then produce a three- to four-page biographical sketch of their individual associated with the Oregon Trail.

ANALYSIS LEVEL

The final level is the *analysis level.* Students take the information collected about their individual and tell his/her story through a historical exhibit. A historical exhibit is an avenue for telling a historical story through images, artifacts, and other primary sources. The selection of sources for the exhibit requires analytical thinking. A three-fold cardboard science board works well for organizing the display.

Students arrange information on the board to tell the story of the person who was researched. Labels and captions should be used creatively with visual images and objects to enhance the message of the exhibit. Teachers may choose to follow the rules of National History Day's historical exhibits and have a limit of 500 words students may use for additional explanation. This includes the text students write for titles, subtitles, captions, graphs, and time lines. National History Day, a premier history education program, provides a detailed explanation of their program and guidelines for students on its web-site (http://www.nhd.org). Historical exhibit evaluation criteria for teachers are also available on National History Day's web-site.

The primary source chosen for this chapter is an image of Ezra Meeker.

Historical Context of Meeker's Childhood

- An image or quote of growing up on a farm in 1830–1840. (Check local historical societies or state historical museums. Most contain diaries, journals, or other primary texts describing life in the nineteenth century.)
- An image or writing of Henry Ward Beecher (Meeker was his paper delivery boy; visit http://digitalgallery.nypl.org)
- A copy of the handbill of *Free Soil, Free Speech, Free Labor, Free Men* in the Indiana newspaper where Meeker worked as a printer's devil (NewspaperArchives.com is one of the services to check for old newspapers)

The Oregon Trail (Early Trips of Ezra Meeker)

- An early map of the Oregon Territory, which included Oregon, Washington, Idaho, Montana, and Wyoming (visit http://digitalhistory.org)
- A copy of the Oregon Donation Land Claim Act (visit http://www.ccrh.org/comm/cottage/primary/claim.htm)
- Ezra Meeker's memorandum of outfits and eatables as appearing on page 15 of ***Seeing the Elephant,*** by Hunsaker. The Oregon Trail (Ezra Meeker's Quest to Preserve the Trail)

- A copy of the cover of his book ***Ox Team Days and the Oregon Trail*** (university libraries have copies, or copies may be purchased for under $10)
- An image or transcript of Ezra Meeker's meeting with Theodore Roosevelt in hope of preserving the Oregon Trail
- The image of Ezra Meeker as an old man

Strategies to Teach Reading

Shared Reading for Older Students

In 1980 Don Holdaway developed and published information concerning shared reading as a technique for helping young children develop reading skills. The idea was to provide students with information and understanding about print conventions and reading that some, but not all, children got at home. Later, intermediate teachers recognized that many of the same benefits could be obtained for older students by adapting the techniques for those age levels. In particular, Janet Allen (2002, Allen and Landaker, 2005) has published books detailing the use of shared reading with middle and high school students.

Shared reading is especially appropriate in overcoming obstacles to student success in reading history, whether it be textbook, information, or fiction. Even students who are adequate readers often come to history class with a lack of interest, insufficient background knowledge, and inadequate vocabulary to fully comprehend the texts they encounter. Shared reading activities can bridge this gap.

Shared Reading versus Reading Aloud

In a shared reading lesson, the teacher reads the text aloud to students. This is a time-proven method for making a text accessible to all students; however, there are a few factors that set shared reading practice apart from standard read-aloud sessions, in which the teacher holds the text and students listen. First, every student must have visual access to the text being read. This can be accomplished through multiple copies of the text (i.e., textbooks, novels, reproducibles), overhead projections, or other large visuals. The students are asked to follow along with their eyes while the teacher reads. In this nonthreatening atmosphere, all students have visual and auditory access to the material, while hearing a model of fluent, meaningful reading.

A second aspect of shared reading is that the material is revisited. In the initial reading, the teacher reads the selected text with as little interruption as possible, pausing only occasionally to explain a word or ask for a prediction. After the piece is read through, the content may be discussed with probing questions. The text will then be reread—perhaps multiple times—in varied ways. Students may read to one another, search the text for interesting or unknown vocabulary words, look for phrases and words pertinent to historical context, separate fact from opinion, and so forth. The combination of fluent modeling and opportunities for students to practice their own reading is powerful in building reading skills.

Texts selected for a shared reading activity should be short and may include poetry, a newspaper or magazine article, a portion or all of a picture book, an interview, a letter or diary entry, or excerpts from a novel or from the textbook. Allen and Landaker (2005) suggests that a variety of shared readings around a single historical topic serves to build much needed background, develop vocabulary, and create interest.

Teaching Activity

Here is a step-by-step outline for a shared reading activity. Our suggested text is the first five paragraphs from chapter 9 of Wadsworth's **Words West.** The title of chapter 9 is "Life, Death, and Accidents."

STEP 1

Prepare multiple copies of the text so that every student has visual access (an alternative is a copy of the text that can be projected so that the whole class can see). Practice reading the text aloud so that a fluent model with appropriate pauses and emphasis will be presented to the students.

STEP 2

Read the text to the class as they follow along visually. After reading, pose some or all of the following questions for discussion:

- What are some ideas about life on the trail that you have as a result of this reading?
- How did people deal with disease and accidents while traveling? Why do you suppose this was so?
- What remedy did you find most unusual? Do you think it would work? Why or why not?
- Why do you suppose people of that time believed in remedies that we find humorous today?

STEP 3

Teach a brief lesson on print conventions that are part of this text. Often students do not understand many common conventions that we take for granted. Being explicit in calling attention to and defining these conventions is helpful to many students.

Ask students where and why they see quotation marks used in the paragraphs. Many students will remark that the quotation marks indicate that someone is speaking. Ask how the author knew to use quotation marks since she probably didn't hear the speaker's actual words (she relied on their written words). Call attention to the phrase "Died of Cholera" in the first paragraph. No one is speaking here. Ask students why quotation marks are used and elicit that this phrase is repeated in the exact words appearing on grave markers, so it is a quote, though not from a specific person.

Also, call attention to the ellipsis used in paragraph 3, "Mother . . . hung." Ask students to explain the use of the repeated periods and tell them it is called an *ellipsis*.

STEP 4

Pair students in groups of two and assign them to reread the five paragraphs. Each student should take a turn reading aloud, while her partner listens. Remind students to use pauses and expression to convey meaning. After two readings, have them turn their papers over and list as many of the common remedies of the time as they can remember. After completing their list, have them refer to their papers and add any remedies that they did not recall. Then ask them to circle words in their lists that are unfamiliar or unknown to them.

STEP 5

As a class, compile a list of common remedies. As words are added to the list, ask students to speculate on the meaning of words, such as *laudanum,* which are likely to be unfamiliar. Teams may be assigned to check dictionaries and encyclopedias for additional information. Conclude the lesson with a discussion of how medical practices are different today and why.

Unit Timeline

- Introduce the Oregon Trail by reading the overview provided in the **Historical Background.**
- Begin the exploratory phase of student research as described in **Strategies to Teach History.** The teacher may wish to post large sheets of paper headed "Food," "Transportation," "Shelter," and so forth. (See the discussion of cultural universals in chapter 2.) Begin each class period with a whole-class read-aloud of a chapter from **Words West,** by Wadsworth. Some or all of these readings may include the shared reading strategy described in **Strategies to Teach Reading.** Assign students to add information to the posted papers in the correct categories. Each student will also keep a list of individuals that he hears mentioned. After the whole-class reading and discussion, students will work independently to read widely in books and on the Internet about the Oregon Trail. The teacher may choose to devote class time to this or may assign this as independent work.
- After students have had a designated period of time to explore information, follow the directions for sharing and choosing a single individual to research further. Students continue research with a narrower focus, as described in **Strategies to Teach History.**
- Finally, students prepare historical displays about their chosen emigrants. Again, this may be done in class or assigned as outside work. The displays can be set up on the designated day as a museum, with students given the opportunity to browse one another's exhibits. The teacher may want to hold students accountable for the browsing by requiring two notes on each display such as information learned, surprising facts, and the like. Students may also nominate and vote for their favorite emigrant, giving reasons for their choices.
- Conclude the study with a class discussion of what the emigrants had in common and how they impacted history.

Adult Bibliography

Dary, David. 2004. ***The Oregon Trail: An American saga.*** New York: Alfred A. Knopf.

Dary presents a carefully researched and comprehensive history of the Oregon Trail, ranging from discovery of the route to the decline of the trail in the late 1800s. Drawing heavily from primary sources, such as diaries and letters, the author explores the experiences of a variety of emigrant groups, including missionaries, the Mormons, and gold seekers as well as the more traditional family groups that traveled the trail at various times. This is a factual and very readable overview of the history of the trail.

McCartney, Laton. 2003. *Across the great divide: Robert Stuart and the discovery of the Oregon Trail.* New York: Free Press.

The story of Robert Stuart is the historical link between the Lewis and Clark expedition and the Oregon Trail. The Corps of Discovery reached the Pacific but failed to find a passage through the Rocky Mountains accessible to wagons. Stuart, a fur trader, discovered South Pass, opening an overland route that over 300,000 emigrants would travel. The biography is extraordinary.

Parkman, Francis. 1996. *The Oregon Trail.* New York: Oxford University Press.

This primary source falls into the category of travel narrative and has been described as the "pre-eminent narrative" of the journey west. The writing is accessible for high school students, and teachers can mine the text for excerpts to illuminate travel west in the mid-nineteenth century.

Student Bibliography

Blos, Joan. 2007. *Letters from the corrugated castle.* New York: Atheneum Books for Young Readers.

Although not specifically about the Overland Trail, this book is appropriate to the period. It offers a detailed view of emigrant life in San Francisco and California during the gold rush days. California and the gold fields were the destination for many travelers on the Overland Trail.

Turner, Ann. 1997. *Mississippi mud: Three prairie journals.* New York: HarperCollins.

A collection of poems in free verse that chronicles the thoughts, fears, and joys of the three oldest children of a pioneer family on their journey from Kentucky to Oregon in the 1800s. This book is very useful in establishing perspective in a readable format.

Wilson, Diane. 2005. *Black storm comin'.* New York: Aladdin Paperbacks.

At almost 300 pages, this book seems long for its audience, with too many twists and turns. However, the characters are well developed and sympathetic and the descriptive writing completely immerses the reader in life on the Overland Trail and in frontier Nevada/California. The work of the Pony Express rider, briefly so important to this period, offers an added dimension.

Web-sites

Additional web-sites of value in supporting student research are listed. Each provides well-researched historical background about the Oregon Trail.

End of the Oregon Trail Interpretive Center, http://www.endoftheoregontrail.org
Library of Congress, American Memory, http://www.memory.loc.gov
New York Public Library, http://www.nypl.org/

The Overland Trail

Oregon: land of milk and honey, rich soil, and opportunity. One popular story circulated in the East was that "in Oregon pigs are running about under the great acorn trees, round and fat, and already cooked, with knives and forks sticking in them so that you cut off a slice whenever you are hungry" (Edward Lenox, 1843). Lured by the promise of better land, better health, gold, adventure, or religious freedom, families packed their possessions in wagons, said good-bye to relatives and friends (perhaps forever), and headed west. Between 1836 and 1870, hundreds, then thousands, of individuals and family groups took to the trail. They were encouraged by a government that promoted the concept of *manifest destiny*—the right of the new nation to expand its borders and claim the rich resources of the West.

The Oregon Trail was never a single, well-defined roadway, but rather, a variety of paths worn through time and use, first by the Native Americans and trappers following game. The discovery of South Pass, a wide, flat area at the continental divide, convinced many that wagon travel was possible. Narcissa and Marcus Whitman, traveling to Washington to establish a mission in 1836, were the first to show that both wagons and women could endure the trip. Travelers headed west from jumping-off points such as Independence and St. Joseph, Missouri, and passed through the present-day states of Kansas, Nebraska, Wyoming, and Idaho. Many continued on to Oregon, but others turned off the main trail at various points for destinations in Utah and California.

The earliest travelers set out with a minimum of information, often incorrect. Some of the first guides were written by people who had not traveled the trails themselves. Although encountering some unexpected and challenging surprises along the way, these early pioneers found land of great beauty, an abundance of game, and generally friendly Native Americans.

What began as a trickle of emigrants in the 1830s swelled to a flood. Later pioneers had more information and were better prepared to face the challenges of the trail. However, other problems surfaced. The endless flow of human and animal traffic had decimated the landscape: cast-off belongings littered the environment, game was scarce, firewood had been burned, and water was polluted. Cholera outbreaks, spread in part by poor sanitary conditions, were common, and graves were a constant feature of the route. Initially friendly, even helpful, Native Americans responded to the destruction of their life and livelihood with sporadic violence.

But still they came. Their purposes were many. Mormons fled religious persecution to seek safety in Utah. Men and women rushed to California in pursuit of gold. Families continued to seek the rainbow of a better life at the end of the trail in Oregon. Although about 1 in 20 of the early pioneers died on the trail, many did indeed reach their goal and establish a new life in the West. The story of the trail is the story of the common man—farmers, merchants, craftsmen—who persevered through incredible difficulties to achieve a better life and, in the process, changed the face of a nation. On the one hand, the trail represents the best of the American character, as pioneers displayed resourcefulness, courage, and fortitude. In other ways, the story is darker, reflecting the Euro-American belief in their own superiority and their inalienable right to claim and use (or abuse) land and resources, without regard for the native populations or for the land itself.

The completion of the Transcontinental Railroad (see chapter 5) in 1869 effectively linked the West Coast with the East and dramatically changed the nature of westward travel. Wagon travel—slow and cumbersome—diminished and died, and the days of the great overland migration were over.

Image of Ezra Meeker

Photo by Roy Norr. Courtesy of WPA.

From *Gateways to Westward Expansion: Using Literature and Primary Sources to Enhance Reading Instruction and Historical Understanding* by Ann Claunch and Linda L. Tripp. Westport, CT: Teacher Ideas Press. Copyright © 2009.

GRAPHIC ORGANIZER

Pre-writing Biographical Sketch

BIOGRAPHICAL SKETCH

Pre-writing graphic organizer for a biographical sketch of the individuals who traveled the Oregon Trail.

Person	NAME:	NAME:	NAME:	NAME:	NAME:	NAME:	NAME:	NAME:	NAME:
What was this person's motivation for traveling the Oregon Trail?									
What was the personal trait(s) that made this person persevere?									
What is the evidence of the trait? Was there an event that happened along the trail or before the journey began to illustrate this character trait?									

CHAPTER 5

The Transcontinental Railroad

Chapter Preview

- **Gateway Books:** *Coolies* by Yin; ***Hear That Train Whistle Blow!*** by Milton Meltzer
- **History Strategy:** Cartoon Analysis
- **Reading Strategy:** Layers of Meaning
- **Historical Background:** The Transcontinental Railroad
- **Primary Source Documents:** "Pacific Chivalry: Encouragement to the Chinese Immigrant"
- **Graphic Organizers:** Cartoon Analysis Worksheet; Layers of Meaning

Gateway Books

Yin. 2001. *Coolies.* New York: Puffin.

In the spirit of this teaching guide, we have chosen to highlight the young adult picture book ***Coolies*** for two reasons. First, the book tells the story of the Transcontinental Railroad from a different voice, that of the Chinese laborers involved in its building. Second, as a fictional text, it allows for the tension between the historical story and the emotional portrayal of a historical event. The book opens with an explanation of the 1850 rebellion in China against the government and the famine that ensued due to political unrest. Many Chinese workers were forced to immigrate to America in search of work.

Throughout ***Coolies,*** the plight of the Chinese worker is woven into the story of two brothers who are working to support their mother and other family members in China. Issues of lower pay (than other workers), dangerous assignments (explosives), and brutal prejudice against the Chinese during the building of the railroad are developed through the text and beautiful watercolor illustrations.

Meltzer, Milton. 2004. ***Hear that train whistle blow!*** New York: Random House.

Milton Meltzer has constructed the story of the American railroad system, from its inception during the Industrial Revolution to the early 1930s, in this nonfiction book for young adults. The complex text deepens the reader's knowledge past the surface level of the time period and stereotypical understanding of robber barons and buffalo slaughters.

Within the story, the great successes of and changes to American life are highlighted, in addition to a discussion of the cost to human lives, to livestock along the routes, and to the land. On reading this Notable Social Studies book, one is reminded that "need is the mother of invention." As America expanded westward, so did the need for rapid travel. The railroad was developed for passenger travel, but a side benefit was the transportation of goods.

The railroad touched every aspect of American life. Meltzer provides a kaleidoscope of travelers on the rail lines. Their voices evoke visual images as the travelers describe their experiences in the railroad cars and cross-country travel of the nineteenth century.

Strategies to Teach History

Cartoon Analysis

Political cartoons ask students to analyze and interpret a hidden text. What seems to be a humorous illustration nudges students to think about how a drawing can convey meaning by exaggerating objects or people, labeling some objects and not others, or placing a symbol to represent a larger concept. Irony, imagery, symbolism, and exaggeration are some of the tools of a political cartoonist.

In the case of the **Primary Source Document** "Pacific Chivalry: Encouragement to the Chinese Immigrant," the artist utilized symbolism in the mountains appearing in the background. These represent Gum Saan, the Mountain of Gold, which symbolized opportunity to the Chinese immigrant. In the foreground, a mining shack and the railroad lines represent the actual work of the Chinese immigrant in the United States. The facial features of the men and the hair queue of the Chinese immigrant are exaggerated to emphasize the difference in appearance and culture. The title of the cartoon draws on irony to make the point that the Chinese are not treated chivalrously. Many more artistic techniques are employed to help the reader understand the point of the cartoon.

Historical Background

When working with political cartoons, students must begin by understanding the historical context. The "Pacific Chivalry" cartoon was published by *Harpers' Weekly*, a periodical appearing between 1857 and 1916. At the time of publication, U.S. immigration policy had shifted dramatically from the open door era to the door ajar period. During the open door era (1820–1880), laws were passed to encourage immigration: the Homestead Act of 1862 and the Immigration Act of 1875. The door ajar era (1880–1920) was characterized by widespread xenophobia. Large numbers of Chinese immigrants arrived and were seen as over-running American culture. They became the subject of racism, culminating in the Chinese Exclusion Act of 1882.

STUDENT ACTIVITY

Distribute a copy of the political cartoon "Pacific Chivalry" to each student. Allow students to look at the cartoon for several minutes, and then ask the following questions:

- What is happening in the cartoon?
- Who are the people represented?
- What is the setting?
- When is this happening? What are the clues allowing you to guess an approximate date?

Divide the students into pairs. Provide each pair with the **Graphic Organizer** at the end of this chapter and review the vocabulary in the left column. Ask students to fold the political cartoon into fourths so that there will be four distinct quadrants. Explain that to understand a political cartoon, one must look carefully at each section of the illustration. As a pair, the students begin with the upper left quadrant and look for the elements listed on the left side of the **Graphic Organizer.** As an element is located, students record the evidence in the appropriate square and then repeat the process for the remaining quadrants.

Sharing

As closure to the lesson, pairs of students take turns sharing with the class the meaning of the cartoon. Extend the discussion by asking students what purpose political cartoons serve.

Extension

If desired, students may be assigned to find a current political cartoon and complete a second **Graphic Organizer.** Findings can be shared at the end of the week, noting likenesses and differences between historical and current cartoons.

Indentured Servant Contract

An additional primary source, a contract for an indentured Chinese servant in the 1880s can be downloaded from www. loc.org. This particular document draws the students' attention to the evolving civil liberties of immigrants to the United States.

Ask students (in small groups) to read the contract and list the "rules for the indentured servants." Emphasize that the person owning the contract could add years of servitude for the smallest infraction of the rules. Follow the reading with a class discussion focusing on the reasons a Chinese immigrant might agree to such terms. Reading the **Gateway Books** listed at the beginning of the chapter will support this discussion.

Extension

Have students research the rights of immigrants today and develop a time line of changes in laws that have served to protect or exploit immigrants to the United States. Students may share their time lines in a classroom display.

Strategies to Teach Reading

Layers of Meaning

Several years ago, we read Eve Bunting's picture book ***Smoky Night*** to a group of fifth graders. Though the story is simple, the book poignantly addresses issues of compassion, tolerance, and race relations. Students sat mesmerized during the story, and when we came to the end, we asked, "What is the author trying to tell us?" Students looked at one another in puzzlement, until one brave soul volunteered, "That he got his cat back." Satisfied nods were evident around the room.

Students, even at middle and high school, are not sophisticated readers. They operate on the basis of a very literal understanding and, unless pushed, do not move beyond the obvious. After the incident described previously and others like it, we began looking for ways to support students in the process of extracting deeper meaning from their reading. We invented and began using the **Layers of Meaning** procedure with picture books and later expanded it to other reading.

Preparation

The "Layers of Meaning" **Graphic Organizer** provided in this chapter may be used in two ways. Most simply, it can be given to students as a single sheet of paper onto which they write headings for each of the concentric squares. To make the organizer even more graphic, we sometimes give students three copies and ask them to cut out the smallest square on one copy and the two smaller squares on a second, while the third is left whole. The cutting should be done carefully so that the outer frames remain intact. The three sheets are then stacked, with the whole sheet on the bottom and the largest frame on top and stapled. When working with a picture book, we ask students to label the outside frame "What I see"; the middle frame "What I hear"; and the center square "What I think."

Sharing the Book

We begin with a picture walk through the book, turning the pages and studying the illustrations. Students take notes on what they notice, recording their observations in the outer "What I see" frame. This is an excellent way to activate students' prior knowledge about a time period and to generate interest in the story. In sharing the book *Coolies* in this way, students often comment on the style of dress, ship travel, cooking and eating around a campfire, labor on the railroad, and the like. After the picture walk observations are completed, we ask students to make predictions about the story. These are often recorded for future reference.

Next we read the story. During the first read-aloud, students simply listen, and we finish the book without extensive discussion. After reading, we instruct students to outline the plot in the middle frame. This is basically a simple, ordered retelling, and we often ask students to number the events as they happened in the story. Students may write the following:

1. There was a famine in China.
2. The brothers traveled to America to earn money for the family.
3. They landed in San Francisco.
4. They went to work on the railroad.

During this process, we emphasize staying with the information or happenings presented by the author. We may reread parts or all of the story if students need this support.

Beyond the Literal Level

The final step, which builds on all that has gone before, is most important. We remind students that authors tell a story for a reason and that our job as readers is to intuit that reason. There is a bigger idea behind a good story that an author wants us to understand; this is the interpretative level. ***Coolies*** develops themes of discrimination, perseverance in the face of obstacles, and family loyalty. Posing provocative questions during this discussion is the teacher's task in leading students to an understanding of these themes. Questions that might be posed after reading ***Coolies*** include the following:

1. Why did the brothers leave China? Have you ever known anyone who traveled to another country for similar reasons?
2. How were the Chinese workers treated by the non-Chinese bosses? Why do you suppose this happened? How did the workers respond?
3. Why do you think the author chose to tell this story? What does she want us to understand about the Chinese workers?
4. What ideas or themes from the story are still present in modern life? How do we see these themes today?

As we lead students through this thinking, we emphasize that not everyone may reach the same conclusion. The goal is not total agreement, but thinking for yourself. At the end of the discussion, we ask students to record their final thoughts in the "What I think" section of their papers.

Extensions

This procedure can also be adapted to informational texts and novels. Instead of a picture walk, we may use the outer frame to consider historical background for an event or a novel. Students who have done a **Windows into the Past** activity (see chapter 2) may summarize their findings here. After reading the text, the middle square is used to fill in the facts: What actually happened? Finally, the central square is used for students to make meaning of the events within the context of the historical background. What conclusions do they reach about the events? What implications do those events have for today? For the future?

Unit Timeline

- Despite the overwhelming popularity of air travel, students of today will have a passing familiarity with railroads and trains. Begin this unit with a "What do you know about trains?" brainstorming session. Simply list any information that students are able to volunteer. This will effectively activate prior knowledge and reveal gaps in their information. Conclude the brainstorm by asking what students know about the history of railroads: When were they established? What were the primary modes of transportation prior to the coming of the railroads (foot travel, horses, wagons)? What advantages did rail travel offer to passengers in this era before cars and planes?
- Read the **Historical Background** on the Transcontinental Railroad. Why was this important? Students who have studied the Oregon Trail will have some idea of the significance of this development.
- Share the picture book ***Coolies*** with the class using the **Layers of Meaning** strategy suggested in **Strategies to Teach Reading.** This book changes the focus of study

from the more general development of the railroads to the more intimate picture of a group of people directly involved in building them.

- Use the political cartoon (**Primary Source Document**) and the indentured papers if desired and follow the suggestions in **Strategies to Teach History** to further explore the attitudes and ideas surrounding Chinese immigration in the nineteenth century. Classes who study both documents can be engaged in a discussion of changing attitudes as the Chinese were first sought after to supply needed labor, particularly on the railroads, and later became objects of fear and discrimination. If time does not permit the entire class to study both documents, the class could be divided in half, with one group looking at the cartoon and the second group studying the indenture papers. Conclude the activity by having each group share their findings.
- Students may go deeper into the history of the era by reading excerpts from *Hear That Whistle Blow!* as shared readings (see chapter 4). Return to the original brainstorm record that began the unit. Ask the students to reconsider, listing what they now know and what questions they still have. The questions may become the focus of additional research, if the teacher so desires.

Adult Bibliography

Ambrose, Stephen. 2001. *Nothing like it in the world: The men who built the Transcontinental Railroad*. New York: Simon and Schuster.

Provides an overview of the time period and is a good resource to use coupled with Michael Murphy's *American Experience: The Transcontinental Railroad, A PBS DVD.* A teacher using the book and the DVD will begin to understand the historical context.

Student Bibliography

Bain, David Howard. 2000. *Empire express: Building the first continental railroad.* New York: Penguin Books.

Comparing and contrasting the first transcontinental railroad, around the Cape of Good Hope, to the American Transcontinental Railroad establishes the gargantuan task of planning, engineering, and completing a railroad spanning an entire continent. By drawing both similarities and distinctions with the American experience, students will achieve a deeper understanding of the feat.

Fine, Jill. 2005. *The Transcontinental Railroad: Tracks across America.* New York: Children's Press.

The author situates the Transcontinental Railroad as one of the premier innovations of the nineteenth century by examining its long-term impact and continuing legacy. This is a high-interest and easy-to-read book for upper elementary students.

Fraser, Mary Ann. 1996. *Ten mile day: And the building of the Transcontinental Railroad.* New York: Henry Holt.

This picture book for older readers celebrates and explores the incredible feat of laying 10 miles of track in a single day. By focusing closely on the events of April 28,

1869, Fraser gives us a slice of American history that illuminates the work and accomplishments of the railroad builders.

Halpern, Michael. 2004. ***Railroad fever.*** New York: National Geographic Children's Book.

Larger print and many illustrations make this book accessible to struggling readers, while providing the content necessary for understanding the Transcontinental Railroad.

Lee, Milly. 2006. ***Landed.*** New York: Farrar, Straus and Giroux.

This turn-of-the-century immigration story follows the experiences of a young Chinese boy coming to America as a paper son, including his detention on San Francisco's Angel Island, in the years following the Chinese Exclusion Act of 1882. The book illustrates the changing attitudes toward Chinese immigration after the completion of the railroad.

Yep, Laurence. 1993. ***Dragon's gate.*** New York: HarperCollins.

In this novel for middle grades, 14-year-old Otter leaves his home in China and follows his father and uncle to America to find work on the Transcontinental Railroad. This engaging story vividly depicts the brutal work of building the railroad, coupled with the prejudice and discrimination faced by the Chinese workers.

The Transcontinental Railroad

The Transcontinental Railroad was completed in six years. It took thousands of workers enduring harsh living conditions and a dangerous work environment to lay over 1,700 miles of track. The work completed the line from Omaha, Nebraska, to Sacramento, California, connecting the East Coast to the West Coast for the first time in American history. This achievement has been deemed as one of the greatest accomplishments of the American people in the nineteenth century.

The Transcontinental Railroad was completed because of the convergence of multiple historical events. On the international stage, the aftermath of the Irish famine and Chinese political unrest had driven young men to immigrate to the United States, providing a large workforce seeking employment. On the national stage, the promise of land and fortune lured more pioneers to the West, which in turn spurred the need for goods and created economic pressures to find a fast way to transport those goods.

The Civil War had ended, and the nation was looking to the future, as the issue of slavery had finally been resolved. The war did more than test the tenets of a young democracy; in the process, it created a workforce of highly skilled engineers and produced a leadership pool of foremen and bosses from the military officers. Need, engineering talent, and workforce brawn made the Transcontinental Railroad possible.

In the construction of the railroad, time was the enemy. The government went into action and passed legislation. In agreement with the Pacific Railroad Act, the Transcontinental Railroad was to be built as quickly as possible. The Civil War also cemented a democracy that allowed for a competitive system between companies, and the Transcontinental Railroad was to be built as a race, with the greatest profits given to the company who laid the track the fastest.

The companies faced overwhelming challenges in the transportation of materials; the engineering feats of crossing gorges, rivers, and mountains; and fending off Indian attacks. These problems were compounded by a lack of laborers in sparsely populated areas. The company that had the biggest muscle power would win: the more men the company could employ, the faster the rails could be laid.

American workers were few because of the isolated location of the tracks, and many were drawn away by the silver rush in Nevada. The Central Pacific, moving the track east, recruited Chinese workers out of California. The Union Pacific, moving the track west, was primarily manned by Irish immigrants.

Workers faced long, hard days and severe racism. The backbreaking work of clearing and leveling the track, carrying heavy loads of rails and rocks, and hammering in 10-inch spikes would begin before sun up and last into the night. In the need to finish quickly, safety was secondary. Accidents, explosions, and even catastrophic loss of human life were expected.

On May 10, 1869, the final tracks were laid joining the Central Pacific and the Union Pacific. The legacy of the Transcontinental Railroad is the transformation of the American frontier and the establishment of urban and rural communities in the western United States.

"Pacific Chivalry: Encouragement to the Chinese Immigrant"

PACIFIC CHIVALRY.

Encouragement to Chinese Immigration.

Courtesy of the Bancroft Library, University of California, Berkeley.

From *Gateways to Westward Expansion: Using Literature and Primary Sources to Enhance Reading Instruction and Historical Understanding* by Ann Claunch and Linda L. Tripp. Westport, CT: Teacher Ideas Press. Copyright © 2009.

Cartoon Analysis Worksheet

The Transcontinental Railroad

Name of the Cartoon	Upper Left	Upper Right	Lower Left	Lower Right	Interpretation: What is the meaning?
Historical Context What clues in the illustration help you know about the time period?					
Symbolism What are the simple objects that stand for the larger concepts?					
Exaggeration What are objects that are over-exaggerated? Clothes? Hair? Facial features?					
Labeling What is the name of the cartoon? What other objects are named?					
Analogy What is being compared in the cartoon?					
Irony What is being distinguished from how things are and how things should be?					

Cartoon Analysis modified from the Library of Congress

From *Gateways to Westward Expansion: Using Literature and Primary Sources to Enhance Reading Instruction and Historical Understanding* by Ann Claunch and Linda L. Tripp. Westport, CT: Teacher Ideas Press. Copyright © 2009.

Layers of Meaning

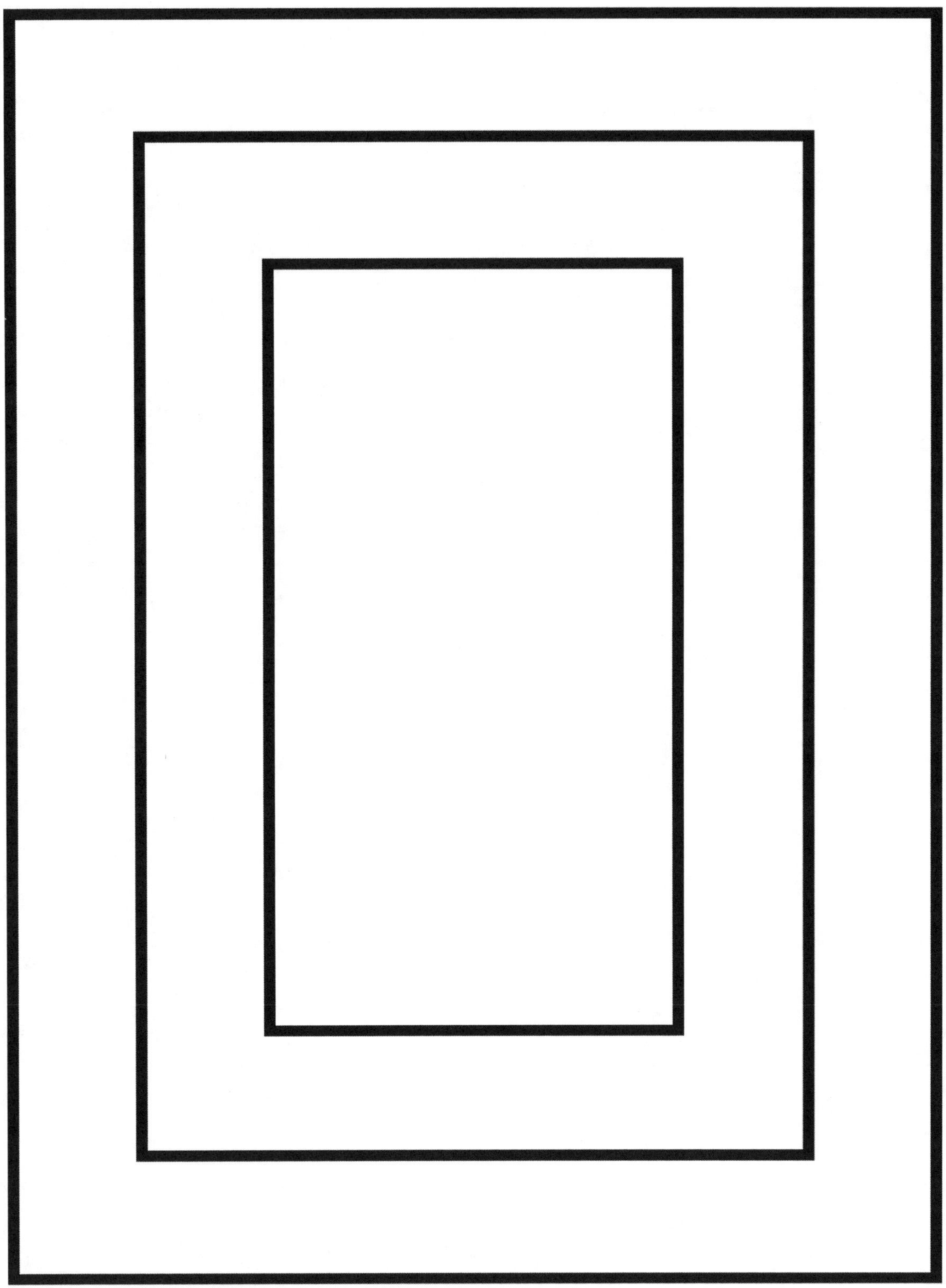

From *Gateways to Westward Expansion: Using Literature and Primary Sources to Enhance Reading Instruction and Historical Understanding* by Ann Claunch and Linda L. Tripp. Westport, CT: Teacher Ideas Press. Copyright © 2009.

CHAPTER 6

The Buffalo Soldiers

Chapter Preview

- **Gateway Books:** *The Buffalo Soldier* by Sherry Garland; *The Forgotten Heroes* by Clinton Cox
- **History Strategy:** Analyzing Correspondence
- **Reading Strategy:** Illustrations in Reading
- **Historical Background:** The Buffalo Soldiers
- **Primary Source Document:** Letter of Recommendation
- **Graphic Organizer:** Reading the Illustrations

Gateway Books

Garland, Sherry. 2006. *The buffalo soldier.* Gretna, LA: Pelican.

Selected as a National Council for the Social Studies Notable Trade Book for 2007, *The Buffalo Soldier* traces the life journey of an unnamed young African American man after the Civil War. In 1866 Congress commissioned six African American regiments of the U.S. Army. For many young African American men, these regiments offered the opportunity to earn income and develop a future with dignity and respect. Some regiments were assigned to duty in the western frontier, where they pursued diverse tasks: protecting stage coaches and mail delivery and telegraph crews and hunting down outlaws and renegades. Native Americans nicknamed these men "buffalo soldiers" because of their perceived resemblance (curly hair and bravery) to the great beasts of the plains.

Told as a first-person account of the details of one man's life stretching from the Civil to the Spanish-American Wars, this book humanizes the buffalo soldier and gives voice to the hopes, dreams, and challenges of this group of people on the American frontier. The rich illustrations of Ronald Himler add another level of historical information and detail.

Cox, Clinton. 1996. *The forgotten heroes: The story of the Buffalo Soldiers.* New York: Scholastic.

In mid-twentieth-century westerns, John Wayne was never flanked by African American riders as the cavalry chased Geronimo. Posses riding to apprehend the notorious outlaw William Bonney, also known as Billy the Kid, did not include African American men. Hollywood movies were historically inaccurate, but the movie industry is not solely responsible for omitting the contributions of African Americans. Images in history textbooks rarely depict a multicultural group inclusive of African Americans in the settlement of the West: the African American frontiersmen, homesteaders, and most important, cavalrymen who opened the Southwest. The buffalo soldiers were a key group who made the frontier safer from Native American raids and guarded the border with Mexico against the Comancheros and Mexican bandits.

The study of the American West has been color-blind with respect to the former African slaves and northern laborers who constructed a new life in the West at the end of the Civil War. *The Forgotten Heroes* is a book that fills the void in history lessons and invites the reader into the journey as the ninth and tenth cavalry evolve from green troops into an elite fighting force.

Clinton Cox introduces readers to the hard lives endured by the buffalo soldiers and the men who distinguished themselves within the group to win the Congressional Medal of Honor. Although their numbers were few—20 percent of the cavalry—the buffalo soldiers in the American West were an integral part of the national story.

Strategies to Teach History

Analyzing Correspondence

In May 1889, paymaster Major Joseph Wham, with an escort from the 24th Infantry and the 9th Cavalry, was ambushed by a band of thieves. Our **Primary Source Document** is Major Wham's letter recommending two buffalo soldiers (Sergeant Benjamin Brown and Corporal Isaiah Mayes) along with six others for the Congressional Medal of Honor, the highest honor given for extreme bravery in battle.

Major Wham's official letter nominating Sergeant Brown and Corporal Mayes for the Congressional Medal of Honor illuminates the dangerous nature of the jobs the buffalo soldiers and other members of the army were engaged in on a daily basis. As we study the buffalo soldiers, we can appreciate the difficulties encountered and the extreme courage of the soldiers through Major Wham's words.

By working with primary sources, official letters, like government records, give us a different view of the event because of the detailed description necessary to convey meaning with little or no emotion attached.

Teaching Activity

After background knowledge of the buffalo soldiers is established, provide the students with a copy of the letter, and also have one projected on a screen, where all students are able to view it. Ask the students to read the letter silently and then aloud with a partner, noting the date of the letter, the name of the sender, and the receiver.

As a class, establish the intent of the letter. Ask students why Sergeant Brown and Corporal Mayes were deserving of the Medal of Honor. In what conditions did their bravery take place? What were the specific actions that occurred to cause General Wham to write the letter?

On completion of the class discussion, ask students to write an official correspondence from the U.S. Secretary of War to Major Wham confirming the presentation of the Medal of Honor to Sergeant Brown and Corporal Mayes. Require students to cite evidence of bravery mentioned in Major Wham's letter and include questions that remain unanswered.

At a later date, the teacher may compile these questions generated by the students as possible research topics.

Working with Correspondence

According to the National Postal Museum, the following guidelines apply to working with historical correspondence:

- As with personal letters, ascertain if your letter has been edited or altered in any way from the original before calling it a primary source.
- If you are analyzing a government document, ask, What is the relationship between the sender and the receiver? What information are they sharing? What information are they leaving out?

Strategies to Teach Reading

Illustrations in Reading

We highly recommend the use of carefully selected picture books with older students (even high school) for a variety of reasons. Generally, the text of a picture book is well suited for a single class period or lesson. A well-developed picture book offers a carefully constructed perspective and an overview of an event, person, or time period with emotional impact. Finally, a well-illustrated picture book offers students a visual entry into the information. This is especially important for second-language learners and struggling readers, although visual reinforcement of the text is beneficial to more fluent readers as well.

What does *well illustrated* mean? First and foremost, it means that the illustrator, like the author, has done research on the time period being presented and is accurate in details of the cultural universals discussed in chapter 2. Furthermore, visual perspectives offer students information that adds to or supports the information in the text. We recently reviewed a number of picture books for teaching students about the national anthem, "The Star-Spangled Banner." More than one of these books was illustrated with designs of exploding fireworks, against which the text was presented. Indeed, the books were beautiful in their colorful presentations, but as a source of information about the meaning or history of "The Star-Spangled Banner" or the historical context in which it was written, they were not useful.

Once an appropriate picture book is chosen, we want students to use the illustrations to develop their understanding of the text, and not as a substitute for reading. A simple lesson using the pictures and guiding students through this process encourages reading, but not relying on the illustrations. Teachers and students who have done work with primary source images, such as paintings and photographs, will see many parallels as the skills are complementary.

Preparation

The teacher begins by selecting one or more pictures from the book for the focus of the lesson. If working with a small group of students who sit close enough to see details, using the picture book itself is appropriate. For larger groups, the teacher may wish to make an overhead or in some way project the chosen image on a wall or screen. The text on the page should be covered at this point. For ***The Buffalo Soldier,*** we have selected and worked with the two-page spread showing the soldiers in school and the later spread of two soldiers in a store. Ronald Himler's illustrations are excellent examples of detailed historical accuracy that can support student learning.

Activity

STEP 1

The lesson may begin with a discussion of the title of the book and a quick picture walk-through of the entire book, allowing comments from students. This helps students begin to activate prior knowledge about the time period. The teacher then returns to the selected pictures for deeper study. If using the **Graphic Organizer** provided in this chapter, reproduce one copy for each student.

STEP 2

Distribute the **Graphic Organizer** or have students prepare a paper divided into three columns. The first column is headed "Observations," the second "Inferences," and the third "Text Information." Ask students to focus on the illustration and describe everything they see in the picture. This is a good point to reinforce the difference between the reading skills of noting details and making inferences. Looking at the illustration of soldiers in school, many students will have a tendency to make global statements such as "they're in church," which are really conclusions. Guide students back to noticing details and describing only what they can actually see in the illustration. Students may benefit from teacher modeling of some of these descriptive phrases. Acceptable responses include, but are not limited to, the following:

- Men wearing uniforms are seated on benches facing a man who is standing.
- One man is holding a book.
- Another man is holding a pencil.
- The rest of the uniformed men are looking at the standing man.

STEP 3

After students have generated several observed details, move them on to "Inferences." Ask students what they think is happening and why they think that. Many students will come back to the idea that the men are in church. Point out that this is, indeed, one possible inference, and ask them to support their conclusion. If there are differing opinions, allow students to discuss these and give their reasons. There is no need for everyone to agree at this point. After discussion, have them record their ideas in the "Inferences" column.

STEP 4

Finally, turn to the reading of the text. The text should either confirm the students' inferences or suggest a different interpretation, that is, that the soldiers are in school learning to read and write. This can provoke discussion of why they needed to learn these skills as adults (most had been slaves) and why they might want to learn now. Have students fill in the third column on "Text Information," noting what the text confirmed or changed about their inferences and any additional information they acquired such as that the learning took place at night, presumably after the day's work, in a schoolroom used by white children during the day.

Depending on the time available, this process can be repeated with other pictures from the text. However, conclude the lesson with a discussion of how text and pictures work together to clarify and build information. Our goal is for students to understand that using the pictures can aid their reading but that not every piece of information can be conveyed visually. Reading the text is critical.

Extension

This procedure, with some adaptation, may also be used when studying illustrated nonfiction. In this case, select one or more particularly pertinent drawings, photographs, or reproductions of artwork. Eliminate the captions and use the three-step process outlined previously to have students describe the illustration, make inferences, and finally, read the captions to confirm their conclusions.

Unit Timeline

- **Illustrations in Reading,** this chapter's strategy for teaching reading, is an excellent way to build background knowledge and understanding of the history of the buffalo soldiers. Follow the procedure for reading the illustrations, which needs to be done before the text is read, then elicit and record student questions about the buffalo soldiers.
- The dream-like illustrations and first-person text of Garland's book invite reading it as a recollection of one who experienced history and is now reliving the past. The text lends itself to multiple reads. After the illustrations have been mined for historical content, read to enjoy the story and then to look beneath the words to understand history.
- Post the student-generated questions in the classroom and then instruct the students to read with a partner the **Historical Background** provided in this chapter. (The teacher may opt to do this as a shared reading, as described in chapter 4.) On completion of reading, ask students to share something new they learned about the buffalo soldiers, and refer again to the student questions. Delete the questions answered by reading the **Historical Background.** Add other questions that have been raised by the additional reading.
- For older students, the teacher may continue the investigation of the buffalo soldiers by assigning *The Forgotten Heroes*. This book is longer and more complex in content presented; therefore the assignment should be stretched over a longer period. Alternatively, the teacher may wish to select chapters or excerpts for study.

Text selections may be read independently or in shared reading (see chapter 4) by the class, depending on the availability of multiple copies and the skills of the students. As the students read, ask each to keep a running list of the names of the buffalo soldiers, the officers, and interesting events. This list may be used for individual research at the end of the unit.

- After reading *The Buffalo Soldier* and *The Forgotten Heroes,* students now have the background to be introduced to the primary source. Complete the activities as described in **Strategies to Teach History.**
- Invite students to discover new information about the buffalo soldiers by engaging in original research. Students may choose a research topic by perusing the list of questions generated by the class or the individual lists kept while reading *The Forgotten Heroes.*

Adult Bibliography

Leckie, William H. 1967. *The buffalo soldiers: A narrative of the Negro cavalry in the West.* Norman: University of Oklahoma Press.

Recognized as the definitive book on the buffalo soldiers, this should be required reading for all teachers presenting units on westward expansion. Leckie explains in detail the Native American conflict in the late nineteenth century and the role the buffalo soldiers played in the Indian Wars.

Schubert, Frank N. 1997. *Black valor: Buffalo soldiers and the Medal of Honor, 1870–1898.* Wilmington, DE: Scholarly Press.

Black Valor presents the names of the 23 buffalo soldiers who distinguished themselves on the battlefield over a period of 20 years. Schubert tells their individual stories, supported by extensive research.

———. 2003. *Voices of the buffalo soldiers.* Albuquerque: University of New Mexico Press.

This book is a compilation of personal and official letters, records, interviews, recollections, and requests written to and from buffalo soldiers. It includes resources such as the report of the battle at Kickipoo Springs, written by Emanuel Stance to his commanding officer, and the sworn, notarized statement of Cathay Williams declaring that she served in the 38th Regiment and was deserving of a pension.

Student Bibliography

Bolden, Tanya. 2003. *American patriots: The story of blacks in the military from the revolution to Desert Storm.* New York: Crown.

This book is adapted from Gail Buckley's award-winning adult version. Filled with inspiring stories, this exceptional text includes the stories of buffalo soldiers Henry Ossain Flipper and Colonel Charles Young.

Flanagan, Alice K. 2005. *The buffalo soldiers.* Minneapolis, MN: Compass Point Books.

The Buffalo Soldiers is a well-written nonfiction book for young historians that includes maps and images of buffalo soldiers and the Native Americans who were their adversaries. The easy-to-read informational book speaks to the tradition of African Americans serving in the military and provides stories of individual buffalo soldiers.

Schlissel, Lillian. 2000. *Black frontiers: A history of African American heroes in the old West.* New York: Aladdin Paperbacks.

Schlissel highlights the role African Americans played in communities of the American West. Through unique historical images and clearly written text, she tells the stories of individuals and families who reconstructed their lives successfully in the frontier. This book will engage and inform students from early elementary to high school.

The Buffalo Soldiers

They were called *buffalo soldiers* by the Comanche and Cheyenne, perhaps in tribute to their bravery and daring. Or perhaps the combination of dark skin, curly hair, and buffalo robes worn for warmth created a physical resemblance to the great creatures of the plains. Whatever the reason, they wore the nickname as they wore the blue uniform of the U.S. Army—with pride. But who were they really?

They were young African American men and, in at least one recorded case, a young African American woman disguised as a man. They were former slaves and the children of slaves, set free by the Emancipation Proclamation. Many had fought with the Union during the Civil War, but others joined the army as a choice made in their new freedom.

The year was 1866—the year after Lee's surrender at Appomattox ended the Civil War. The U.S. Congress passed legislation creating the first all–African American cavalry and infantry units. Recruitment offices were established in New Orleans, Louisiana, and in Kentucky. Recruits were promised pay of $13 per month plus room, board, and clothing. To men with few other options for gainful employment in a society that ignored or openly hated them, it seemed an opportunity.

Two cavalry units were formed and sent west. The 9th Cavalry went to Ft. Leavenworth, Kansas, the 10th to Texas and, later, New Mexico. Their task was to keep peace on the frontier, controlling outlaws, hostile Native Americans, and Mexican revolutionaries. They performed dangerous work in a harsh environment against extremes of weather, desert thirst, and a roster of adversaries, including Geronimo, Sitting Bull, Victorio, Lone Wolf, Billy the Kid, and Pancho Villa. It was these units that came to be known as buffalo soldiers.

The work of these young men was vital in the settlement of the West. In addition to establishing law and order, they explored and mapped large areas of the Southwest, built and maintained forts, and protected the railroad crews and the stage and mail routes.

Daily life was hard. Frontier barracks were little more than hovels—home to rats, mice, snakes, and cockroaches. Bathing was done in the local creeks that were also a source of water for drinking and cooking. Diseases such as dysentery, bronchitis, and diarrhea were common. Food was plentiful, but without variety: beef or bacon, beans, potatoes, and vegetables in season. There might be an occasional treat of fruit or jam. Soldiers worked seven days a week. The only holidays were Christmas and the Fourth of July. Patrols away from camp often lasted six months; time in base camp involved daily drills and parades. Leisure activities were limited. African American men were not generally welcome in local communities and were sometimes shunned even by the white officers who commanded them. Many spent what free time they had learning to read and write, skills that had been denied to them as slaves.

Despite these drawbacks, the buffalo soldiers performed their mission with bravery and honor. Over the years, several were awarded the Congressional Medal of Honor and won the respect of many white commanders and fellow soldiers. They were instrumental in the taking of San Juan Hill in Cuba in 1898 and paved the way for other African American regiments in World War I and World War II. The order ending segregation in the U.S. armed forces was signed by President Harry S. Truman in 1948.

Letter of Recommendation

Pay Department, US Army

Tucson Arizona, Sept. 1, 1889

To the Secretary of War
Washington, D.C.
Thro. Hdgrs. Dept. of Arizona

Sir,

Referring to the fact that while en route from Fort Grant to Fort Thomas May 11 last, making a payment on the April muster, my party was ambushed and fired into a number of armed brigands, since estimated by U.S. Marshall Meade at from twelve to fifteen, but by myself and entire escort, two non-commissioned officers and nine privates at from fifteen to twenty.

A large boulder, weighing several tons, had apparently, as is often the case, rolled into the road and stopped, my ambulance (coach) had almost reached this boulder when it closely came to a halt, and to my question, "What's the matter sergeant?" came his immediate response from the box, "A boulder on the road sire." The sergeant stopped, passing armed down the gorge to the point to clear the way.

They were nearly at the boulder when a signal shot was fired, which was instantly followed by a volley believed by myself and entire party to be fifteen or twenty shots.

A sharp, short fight, lasting something over thirty minutes, ensured, during which time the following officers and privates, eight of which were wounded, two being shot twice, behaved in the most courageous and heroic manner . . . .

. . . Sergeant Benjamin Brown, though shot through the abdomen, did not quit the field until again wounded, this time through the arm . . . .

. . . Corporal Mayes, then without my knowledge walked and crawled two miles to the Cottonwood ranch and gave the alarm to Barney Norton.

AGO, General Correspondence File, 1890-1017, RG 94, NARA (M-9292, roll 2)

Reading the Illustrations

Observations	*Inferences*	*Text Information*

CHAPTER 7

Indian Boarding Schools

Chapter Preview

- **Gateway Books:** *Sweetgrass Basket* by Marlene Carvell; *The Ledgerbook of Thomas Blue Eagle* by Jewel H. Gutman and Gay Matthaei; *Julia Singing Bear* by Jewel H. Gutman and Gay Matthaei
- **History Strategy:** Analyzing Photographs; Analyzing Quotes
- **Reading Strategy:** Word Splash
- **Historical Background:** The Indian Boarding Schools
- **Primary Source Documents:** Carlisle Indian School Photographs; Indian School Quotes
- **Graphic Organizer:** Quote Analysis Chart

Gateway Books

Carvell, Marlene. 2005. *Sweetgrass basket.* New York: Dutton.

Mattie and Sarah, Mohawk sisters of 12 and 14, leave their home near the St. Lawrence River to attend the Carlisle Indian School. It is a choice that their father believes to be in their best interest after the death of their mother. At the school, they find both friends and enemies, kindness and cruelty, as they struggle to deal with the demands of their new life.

The quiet voices of the two sisters alternate speaking to us from the pages of this middle grade and older novel. As readers, we share their heartbreaking homesickness and loneliness. We feel the humiliation they experience as their Indian heritage is denied and belittled. We see as well the unexpected kindnesses and friendship of their days at the Indian School. This book connects us to the reality of the Indian schools, showing the good intentions beside the often cruel practices.

Gutman, Jewel H., and Gay Matthaei. 1994. *The ledgerbook of Thomas Blue Eagle.* Charlottesville, VA: Thomasson-Grant.

Like a soft whisper across time, the simple prose of *The Ledgerbook of Thomas Blue Eagle* evokes for us a life very different from our own, yet equally to be respected and honored. *The Ledgerbook of Thomas Blue Eagle* is a fictionalized first-person narrative of a boy growing up in the traditional ways of an Oglala Sioux warrior in the mid-1800s: riding his horse, hunting buffalo, counting coup. Blue Eagle's life changes dramatically after the defeat of his people at Wounded Knee, when he is taken to the Carlisle

(Pennsylvania) Indian School. His traditional Sioux finery is discarded, his hair is cut, and he is forced to learn English. The style of this book is based on actual ledger books created by Native American students at the Carlisle School. The illustrations are in the form of Native American picture stories.

Gutman, Jewel H., and Gay Matthaei. 1995. *Julia Singing Bear.* Charlottesville, VA: Thomasson-Grant.

    Julia Singing Bear is a companion work to *The Ledgerbook,* told from the point of view of an Oglala Sioux female transitioning from her traditional childhood to the dominant Anglo world. As a young girl, Singing Bear and her grandparents rescue and heal an army expedition photographer after he falls from a mountain ledge. In gratitude, he presents Singing Bear with an album of photographs. At Carlisle Indian School, she takes the name Julia, learns to read and write, and adds the text, as well as additional photographs, to her story. This longer, denser text includes more detail than the previous book.

    Both books give us glimpses into the social and cultural structure of the Oglala Sioux and illustrate, through example, the sharp distinction between life in the village and life at the Carlisle Indian School. Readers are challenged to consider the dichotomy of names, for example, contrasting the tribal name bestowed by a vision with the random choice of a common Anglo name from a chalkboard list provided by the Indian School.

    The Ledgerbook of Thomas Blue Eagle and *Julia Singing Bear* are written in consultation with Arthur Amiotte, a Lakota studies professor and Oglala tribal member.

Strategies to Teach History

Since the point of contact, 1492, the prevalent attitude toward the Native Americans by the Europeans was one of subjugation. Through active assimilation practices like the suppression of religion and languages and through government policies, the Native American nations were under siege throughout the first 400 years of contact.

By the latter part of the nineteenth century, as the desire for farming and ranching land increased, the need to assimilate Native Americans reached a peak. There were different perspectives on the Native American solution. One was extermination, but the dominant one was to "save" the Native American by providing the tools, language, white work ethic, and vocation necessary to be successful in American culture. This re-education would provide the Native Americans with a different livelihood—domestic work for the women and trades for the men—which in turn would free traditional native lands for settlement.

Richard Pratt, a person with a passion for "saving" the Native Americans, began a campaign to transform Native Americans by a "total immersion program" through the education system. His plan was to create Indian boarding schools to re-educate Native American students to the ways of main-stream society. Although Indian boarding schools had been in existence since the late 1700s, under Pratt's plan, Native American children were voluntarily and forcibly removed from their families and placed in schools far from their homes, with the purpose of erasing the "Indian" and creating in appearance and attitude a "white" American.

Analyzing Photographs

The Carlisle Indian School systematically used photography to document the progress of assimilation. As groups of students arrived, they were photographed. The purpose of the photographs was to provide evidence of the success of the assimilation, at least in appearance. Our primary sources are two photographs from the Carlisle Indian School in 1887. Both photographs feature the same 12 Apache children. Image 1 was taken on arrival at the train station. Image 2 shows the group after four months at the school.

Project Image 2 onto the screen first, where all students may see. This is the photograph of the Native Americans after they have been at the school for four months. Beginning with this image helps the students to look very closely. Examine the second image and ask the students to discuss the photo through a series of questions:

- What can you tell about the historical time period?
- What Native American nation is represented?
- What emotions are portrayed by the people in the image?

Next show Image 1. Ask the students to answer the same questions and then talk about when each of the photos was taken and for what purpose.

Analyzing Quotes

Copy the **Graphic Organizer** and the **Primary Source Document** with the quotes for each student. Ask students to read the quotes silently several times. Have the students respond emotionally to the quotes by asking the following:

- How did the quotes make you feel?
- Which quote do you agree with and why?
- Which quote do you disagree with and why?

Next, look objectively at the quotes. Assign pairs of students to different quotes and ask them to complete the **Graphic Organizer** for this chapter. Compile their responses on a chart for the entire class.

After completing the **Graphic Organizer** and photo analysis, assign students to gather more information about the Indian schools of the late 1800s by reading one of the nonfiction books listed in the **Student Bibliography** at the end of the chapter.

Strategies to Teach Reading

Word Splash

A **Word Splash** is a pre-reading activity that can accomplish several purposes, including introducing vocabulary, activating prior knowledge, and engaging interest and motivating students to read. In addition, a **Word Splash** is easy to prepare and present.

Preparation

The teacher selects 8 to 12 words from a one- or two-page text or short picture book to be read by the students. The words may be nouns, verbs, adjectives, or adverbs and should represent important ideas in the text. Short phrases are also acceptable. The title or subject of the text is written in the center of a whiteboard or chalkboard placed in front of the class. The selected words are randomly splashed or scattered around the title. Placing the words at diagonals to the title and to one another predisposes the brain to make new connections.

If using the **Historical Background** "Indian Boarding Schools" for this chapter, that title should go in the center of the board. Words surrounding the title might be *traditional, locomotive, whitening, Lakota, students, exterminated, discarded, Richard Henry Pratt,* or "Kill the Indian, save the man." These selections mix single words with phrases and include proper nouns, adjectives, and verbs. The list also contains words that will be familiar to students as well as some that may be more challenging.

Student Activity

Students may complete the activity as individuals, partners, or in small groups, at the discretion of the teacher.

Instruct students to write sentences using the words splashed around the title. Each word must be included in a sentence, but a single sentence can contain more than one of the posted words. Each sentence should refer to the topic indicated by the title, linking the words to the text and to one another.

After completing the sentences, students read the text, underlining or marking with sticky notes the words as they come to them. Students are usually eager to read to discover if their guesses about the words were correct. After reading, students compare their sentences to the text for accuracy of ideas, marking their sentences as true or false, based on their reading. False sentences should be rewritten to be correct.

Closure

Close the activity with a class discussion asking students to identify information they confirmed or ideas they changed based on their reading. Students are often surprised at the way in which their minds made connections that approached the correct understanding. The teacher may wish to make the point that we often know more than we think we know about any given topic and that we can make connections that make sense to ideas already in our mental computers.

Unit Timeline

- The study of the before and after photographs of Carlisle Indian School students can both provoke student interest and provide emotional and informational background for the study of Indian boarding schools. Begin this unit with the study of the **Primary Source Document** "Carlisle Indian School Photographs," as described in **Strategies to Teach History.**

- Continue with the study of the **Primary Source Document** "Indian School Quotes," as described in **Strategies to Teach History.**
- Complete the **Word Splash** activity from **Strategies to Teach Reading** and have students read (independently, in partners, or as a whole class) the **Historical Background** for this chapter.
- Use the literature selections to extend students' understanding of the boarding school experience from the point of view of the Native Americans. *Sweetgrass Basket* is an excellent choice for read-aloud or novel study groups. *The Ledgerbook of Thomas Blue Eagle* and *Julia Singing Bear* are also excellent read-aloud choices, if time is more limited.

Adult Bibliography

Child, Brenda J. 1993. *Boarding school seasons: American Indian families, 1900–1940.* Lincoln: University of Nebraska Press.

Child uses interviews, letters from children, and archival sources to describe boarding school life from the perspective of former students and their families.

Coleman, Michael C. 1993. *American Indian children at school, 1850–1930.* Jackson: University Press of Mississippi.

Native American autobiographies from many published sources give an overview of life at the boarding schools.

Lee, Lanniko, et al. 2002. *Shaping survival: Essays by four American Indian tribal women.* Lanham, MD: Scarecrow Press.

This book covers the educational experiences of four American Indian women who were educated in schools such as the Bureau of Indian Affairs boarding schools, off-reservation public schools, and Indian mission schools.

Student Bibliography

Bruchac, Joseph. 2006. *Jim Thorpe: Original all-American.* New York: Dial Books for Young Readers / Penguin Young Readers Group.

Noted author Bruchac uses first-person narrative to tell the life story of one of the Carlisle Indian School's best known graduates. Thorpe was an outstanding athlete from an Oklahoma tribe who also won Olympic gold. This 2007 Notable Book in the Social Studies will be of interest to young adult readers.

Bunting, Eve. 1995. *Cheyenne again.* New York: Clarion Books.

This picture book details the feelings and struggles of a young Cheyenne who is taken from his home and people to learn the "white man's ways."

Freedman, Russell. 1983. *Children of the wild West.* New York: Scholastic.

Freedman's book includes a chapter on American Indians that contrasts the childhood tasks, pleasures, and expectations of Indian children with those of pioneer children.

He discusses the impact of white settlement on Indian life and the institution of the Indian schools. The book is illustrated with actual photos of the time.

MacDonald, Flora. 1992. ***Plains Indians.*** New York: Barrons.

Absorbing illustrations, maps, insets, foldouts, diagrams, and photos serve to provide a wealth of information on the origins, societies, cultures, and destruction of the Plains Indians.

The Indian Boarding Schools

As the locomotive steamed into the station at Carlisle, Pennsylvania, townspeople gathered around the tracks, hoping to get a glimpse of the passengers—children from the Dakota Territory. They stepped from the train, wrapped in their blankets, hair long and loose or braided. The children were Lakota, called *Sioux* by Euro-Americans, who regarded them as "wild" and foreign objects of curiosity. Probably they were tired, hungry, anxious or frightened, and homesick for family. They were the first students of the newly founded Carlisle Indian Industrial School.

In a matter of days, these children would look very different. Their long hair would be cut short. Their traditional clothing and finery would be discarded—burned—and they would be dressed in stiff, tight-fitting shoes, with pinafores for the girls and uniforms for the boys. Even their names would be changed. The goal was to make them as "white" as possible.

The architect of these changes was Richard Henry Pratt, founder and superintendent of the new (in 1879) Carlisle Indian School. Pratt began his military career in the West as an officer of the 10th Cavalry, the buffalo soldiers. Later, he was in charge of a military prison in St. Augustine, Florida, for Indian "hostiles" brought from their western homes to lessen their influence on their tribes and to make escape unlikely.

Pratt was considered something of a forward thinker for his time. Like the Indian reformers (mostly Quakers), he did not want to see Native Americans exterminated. His mission was to "civilize" them and prepare them to be a part of white society. How? By turning them into darker-skinned copies of white men and women. He believed that this could be most effectively done if started at an early age (childhood), far away from the influences of the tribe. Thus the Indian boarding school was born. His philosophy was "Kill the Indian, save the man."

While a few Native Americans agreed to send their children to the schools to learn English, many children were forcibly removed from their families. Their time at the school was divided between learning academics (math and reading) and practicing trades (blacksmithing, carpentry, sewing). School life was conducted in a very military manner, with marching and drills. Discipline was harsh, sometimes cruel. Children could have their mouths washed with lye soap for speaking their native language or be locked in a cell for trying to go home. Some tried to run away, but they were far from home and had few resources. Many became ill and died at the school without ever seeing their families again. Others survived and returned to their tribes, changed forever.

The Indian schools were an outgrowth of westward expansion. As more and more white settlers streamed into the West, the Indians became an obstacle to be removed. One solution was to force the Native Americans onto reservations. Another was to eliminate their culture and traditional ways so that they would be more acceptable and less threatening to their white neighbors.

Although Carlisle Indian School was the first and the most famous of the Indian schools, others followed. A few still exist today. Over the years, the style of the schools changed. They became more humane, more focused on education, and less intent on "whitening" the Native children. Some students reported positive experiences: they experienced better living conditions than they had at home, learned new skills, met members of other tribes and groups, and formed lasting friendships. For most, however, the experience was negative, if not traumatic. Many, if not most, felt intense loneliness separated from their families and, ultimately, from their tribal identities in a melting pot of "Indianness" and were continually reminded of their supposedly inferior status.

Some graduates of the Indian schools went on to literary and athletic success, but many discovered that they no longer belonged anywhere—not as Indians, not as white men.

Carlisle Indian School Photographs

Image 1. Chiricahua Apaches as they arrived at Carlisle from Fort Marion, Florida, November 4, 1886. Front row let to right, Celement Seanilzay, Beatrice Kiahtel, Janette Pahgostatun, Margaret Y. Nadasthilah, and Federick Eskelsejah. Second row, Humphrey Escharzay, Samson Noran, and Basil Ekarden. Third row, Hugh Chee, Bishop Eatennah, and Ernest Hogee. Courtesy of the Cumberland County Historical Society, Carlisle, PA.

Image 2. Chiricahua Apaches four months after their arrival at Carlisle, March 1887. Front row, left to right, Humphrey Escharzay, Beatrice Kiahtel, Janette Pahgostatun, Bishop Eatennah, and Basil Ekarden. Second row, Ernest Hogee and Margaret Y. Nadasthilah. Third row, Samson Noran, Federick Eskelsejah, Celement Seanilzay, and Hugh Chee. Courtesy of the Cumberland County Historical Society, Carlisle, PA.

Indian School Quotes

"The common schools are the stomach of the country in which all people that come to us are assimilated within a generation.

When a lion eats an ox, the lion does not become an ox but the ox becomes a Lion."

Henry Ward Beecher

"If the Great Spirit had desired me to be a white man, he would have made me so. He put in your heart certain wishes and plans: in my heart he put others and different desires. Each man is good in the sight of the Great Spirit."

Sitting Bull, Teton Sioux

" Kill the Indian, Save the man."

R.H. Pratt's philosophy as posted at the Carlisle Indian School in the 19th century

From *Gateways to Westward Expansion: Using Literature and Primary Sources to Enhance Reading Instruction and Historical Understanding* by Ann Claunch and Linda L. Tripp. Westport, CT: Teacher Ideas Press. Copyright © 2009.

Quote Analysis Chart

The Indian Boarding Schools

	Henry Beecher	Sitting Bull	Richard Pratt
What is the purpose of the quote?			
Who is the intended audience for the quote?			
What do you know about the historical time period of the quote? How is the historical time period reflected in the quote?			
What emotions does the quote raise in present-day society and why?			

CHAPTER 8

Cowboys and Longhorns

Chapter Preview

- **Gateway Books:** *Cowboy Ghost* by Robert Newton Peck; *The Journal of Joshua Loper* by Walter Dean Myers; *Cowboys and Longhorns* by Jerry Stanley
- **History Strategy:** Song Analysis
- **Reading Strategy:** Word Origins
- **Historical Background:** Cowboys and Longhorns
- **Primary Source Document:** Song, "Git Along Little Dogies"
- **Graphic Organizer:** Semantic Feature Analysis

Gateway Books

Peck, Robert Newton. 1999. *Cowboy ghost.* New York: HarperCollins.

Titus Timothy MacRobertson (Tee) is 16 in 1924, when he accompanies his older brother and the Spur Box ranch hands in driving a cattle herd to market. Tee narrates the saga of long, boring days in the saddle, punctuated with storms, stampedes, and even death, as he struggles to prove himself equal to the task and to gain the recognition of his father.

Although this cattle drive takes place in the scrub country of central Florida (historically accurate), rather than in the West, this coming-of-age novel is exceedingly faithful to the cowboy experience. Filled with humor, sorrow, and gritty realism, and peppered with colorful cowboy language, this book offers students an authentic and engaging picture of cowboy life.

Myers, Walter Dean. 1999. *The journal of Joshua Loper: A black cowboy.* New York: Scholastic.

This story of a young cowboy's first cattle drive on the Chisholm Trail in 1871 offers younger (upper elementary and middle school) and less experienced readers a well-researched and engaging narrative of cowboy life. Readers must accept the somewhat unlikely conceit that a young trail hand on his first drive would keep a journal (explained in the book). On the other hand, the use of an African American protagonist reminds readers that cowboy life and trail drives were multi-ethnic and multi-cultural, contrary to typical Hollywood depictions. Joshua's experiences of trail life are authentic and realistic, though not as graphic as the preceding selection.

Stanley, Jerry. 2003. ***Cowboys and longhorns.*** New York: Crown.

Stanley rejects the romanticized myth of the cowboy created by the media and offers instead a detailed look at real cowboys and their work. This is no prettified picture, but rather describes a job that was difficult, dangerous, and lonely.

Who was this character called the cowboy? Stanley answers, "At the start, he was Mexican and African American, later he was an Anglo. Typically, he was a greenie who was overworked, underpaid, often bored and sometimes terrified. He was sleepy. He was sore. He didn't like nonwhites, swore on nearly every occasion, and blew his pay on alcohol and other diversions. If he didn't die in the work, he quit after one drive. He didn't like being a cowboy" (p. 37).

The story of the American West is also the story of the longhorn, wild crossbreeds that developed in the West Texas plains. Without the longhorn, there would have been no need for the cowboy. These fierce, independent, hardy cattle and the tough men who sought to corral and control them forged a relationship in which each shaped and changed the life of the other.

In eight chapters, Stanley traces the yearly cycle of the cow hunt, the long drive, and the end of the trail that described the cowboy life. Illustrated primarily with photographs, this book for middle grades and high school readers paints a gritty, realistic picture of the life of a workingman of the American West.

Strategies to Teach History
Song Analysis

The Western myth of the lone cowboy singing a song as he rides his horse off into the sunset is one that is often romanticized in Hollywood films. In reality, the cowboy did not sing for entertainment, but rather as a practical strategy to keep awake, and possibly to soothe the herd. The work of the cowboy was hard and dangerous. The hours were long and the cattle were unpredictable. While working with a herd of 3,000 cattle—the average size of a herd on the cattle drive—the workday lasted from before sunrise to late in the evening. Long hours in the saddle and isolation from one another led to an understandable state of fatigue and loneliness. The song might be one composed about a cowboy's surroundings or from a popular tune from the time period.

Most men lasted an average of four months as a full-time cowboy. The type of men who gravitated to the life of the cattle drives were young men looking for work and adventure. Most were illiterate. The average cowboy did not keep a diary or write home about his experiences. For this reason, we have few first-hand accounts of life on the trail. Cowboy songs offer us a glimpse into the life of the cowboy.

Song Selection

When choosing a song as a source, be sure to note the date the song was written. Is it a primary source, created during the time period you are investigating, or a secondary source written later? Further research may reveal that the song was composed much earlier than it was published in print form.

Teaching Activity

Distribute the words to the cowboy song "Git Along Little Dogies" (see the **Primary Source Document**). If possible, play the song as a recording or invite a student to play the song on a musical instrument. If you Google music for "Git Along Little Dogies," several web-sites offer to download the music for under $2. The book ***Cowboy and Western Songs: A Comprehensive Anthology,*** which appears in the bibliography at the end of this chapter, has music notation along with the historical background of the song.

Caution the students that songs are a creative source, and like a painting, they may be embellished or changed over time. The text used for this version of "Git Along Little Dogies" was taken from an 1893 journal. Ask students to listen to the music, read the words silently, and then discuss with the class the historical connection with the song. "Git Along Little Dogies" mentions elements of trail life such as the bedground, spurs, and motivations for becoming a cowboy.

After students have read and listened to the cowboy song, project the words onto a screen, where all students may see, and ask students to consider the following questions:

1. Who would sing the song?
2. Where might the song be sung?
3. What is the message the song is trying to convey? What is the historical significance?
4. What is the tone of the song? How does the tone reflect the culture of the singer?
5. What three things have you learned about cowboys from the song?

After students analyze the lyrics of "Git Along Little Dogies" for historical information, assign the students to research information about Owen Wister. Excerpts read from ***The Virginian*** (available through most public libraries) reveal the romantic version of western life: strong, silent strangers riding into the West to bring order to chaos, to tame outlaws, and to save the schoolmarm. Information gained about Owen Wister, "Git Along Little Dogies," and ***The Virginian*** can be contrasted with the real life of the cowboys in the fiction and nonfiction books highlighted in this chapter.

Extension

Using the source of the songs, like ***Cowboy and Western Songs: A Comprehensive Anthology*** by Austin E. Fife and Alta S. Fife, assign students, in small groups or individually, to choose another cowboy song and research the origins and the historical connection and significance of the words. When the research is complete, students may transform their research into a historical presentation of the history of their song. Extra points are always awarded for singing!

Strategies to Teach Reading

Word Origins

English is an eclectic language, having borrowed and incorporated words from many sources into its lexicon. Due to the influence of the Mexican vaqueros, cowboy language is filled with connections to and corruptions of Spanish words. Exploring these connections allows all students to better understand the roots of the English language and builds a sense of pride and increased language skills for second-language learners who are native speakers of Spanish. The following suggested activity could be done at various points in the unit; however, we like to complete this more in-depth study after students have had some exposure to information about cowboys and to the vocabulary of cowboy life.

Teacher Preparation

Copy the **Graphic Organizer** "Semantic Feature Analysis," providing one copy for each student. If doing a simplified version of this activity, have students divide a paper into three columns marked "Spanish Word," "English Word," and "Definition." Provide the following list on a chalkboard or whiteboard and have students copy the list in the left-hand column of their papers. (Note that the **Graphic Organizer** already has this list in the first column):

1. botas
2. bronco
3. chapparreras
4. chaqueta
5. espuelas
6. lazo
7. mesteño
8. rancho
9. la reata
10. vaca
11. vaquero

Teaching Activity

STEP 1

Tell students that these are Spanish words related to cowboy life. Ask students to speculate about the words' meanings and pronunciations. Students who are speakers of Spanish may provide pronunciation, but ask them to withhold their translations at this point.

STEP 2

Provide the following list of English words (without Spanish translations) on another paper, on an overhead, or on the board. Have students match each word in the following list to a word in the original list. Students should complete this matching with little additional instruction from the teacher:

- lariat (la reata)
- bronco (bronco)
- jacket (chaqueta)
- lasso (lazo)
- cow (vaca)
- ranch (rancho)

- spurs (espuelas)
- chaps (chapparreras)
- buckaroo (vaquero)
- mustang (mesteño)
- boots (botas)

STEP 3

After the task is completed, discuss the strategies they used to find matches. If students are completing the "Semantic Feature Analysis" worksheet, they should check off each feature that applies to individual words. Words can then be grouped into categories according to their similarities and differences such as words that are incorporated into English with little or no change (bronco, ranch); words that retain spelling and pronunciation similarities because English speakers corrupted the original pronunciation (*vaquero* to buckaroo, *chaqueta* to jacket); or words that were shortened (chaps for *chapparreras*). Words can also be discussed in meaning groups such as clothing, tools, places, and so forth. If working with the definitions suggested next, this step may be saved until after step 4.

STEP 4

Extend the activity by asking students to match the following definitions to the word pairs. Definitions are listed here to correspond to the numbered words in the first list in the previous section. Definitions should be presented to students in mixed order:

1. leather shoes that extend up the leg
2. a wild, unbroken horse
3. leather leg covering worn over trousers for protection
4. a garment for the upper body
5. a sharp, pointed device secured to the rider's heel, used to prod the horse
6. a long rope with a noose at the end
7. a wild horse
8. a farm or land area used for cattle raising
9. a rawhide rope
10. cow
11. cowboy or ranch hand

If not done previously, ask students to now list the words in meaning groups and label the groups. For example, *botas* (boots), *chaqueta* (jacket), and *chapperreras* (chaps) are all clothing, while *la reata* (lariat), *espuelas* (spurs), and *lazo* (lasso) are tools that cowboys used in their work. Once the word groups have been composed and labeled, ask students what words they might add.

Closure

Conclude the word study with a class discussion of why words are borrowed from different languages to become part of common usage and how words change over time.

Students can also consider how certain occupations develop a specific vocabulary or jargon related to the job.

Unit Timeline

- Begin with a whole group brainstorm around the topic "cowboys"; this may be simply a large poster with "cowboys" in the center. Encourage students to share what they know or think they know about cowboys, trail drives, and cattle. An alternate suggestion would be to simply list cowboy vocabulary, asking students what words they associate with cowboys.
- If time permits, read one of the **Gateway Book** fiction selections. This may be a read-aloud or novel study for class groups. If time is short, share a picture book from the **Student Bibliography** section. After reading, return to the initial chart and highlight ideas or vocabulary confirmed. Add any information about cowboys that is new in a different color.
- Read the **Historical Background** page on "Cowboys and Longhorns" as a shared reading (see chapter 4). Alternatively, this page may be read independently or by small groups of students. Again, confirm or add information to the chart created initially.
- Use the suggestions in **Strategies to Teach History** to study cowboy music. Ask students to think about how the songs confirm or offer new information.
- Complete the **Word Origins** activity in **Strategies to Teach Reading.**
- Conclude the unit with a class discussion on the myth of the cowboy. If time permits, show the class *Hondo* (1953) with John Wayne or *The Indian Fighter* (1956) with Kirk Douglas. Ask students to view the film with the objective of separating fact from fiction. They will need to think about the reality of cowboy life as opposed to that presented, and to consider what, in fact, cowboys really did contribute to the settlement of the frontier.

Adult Bibliography

Fife, Austin E., and Alta S. Fife. 1971. *Cowboy and western songs: A comprehensive anthology.* Ojai, CA: Creative Concept.

This is an excellent resource for teachers working with cowboy songs. The anthology provides 200 songs subdivided into 14 sections such as "Westerners at Work" and "Treacherous Women." Some historical background is given for each song. Music notation is provided.

Katz, William Loren. 2005. *The black West: A documentary and pictorial history of the African American role in the westward expansion of the United States.* New York: Harlem Moon.

An under-used resource by teachers, *The Black West* presents unsung heroes such as Bill Pickett, who created a new way of bulldogging by biting steers on the lip, and Mary Fields, the first African American woman stagecoach driver in Montana, as well as many others. This is a well-researched, easy-to-read, informative book.

Wister, Owen. 1935. *The Virginian.* New York: Grosset and Dunlap.

Written in 1902, this book started a new western genre. The young, beautiful but helpless school teacher is rescued by the handsome but coarse westerner. The storyline became prevalent in the twentieth century westerns.

Student Bibliography

Freedman, Russell. 1985. *Cowboys of the wild West.* New York: Clarion.

Although an older title, this book has outstanding photographs and is highly recommended for any unit of study about cowboys. Through text and illustrations, the book shows the reader the physical demands of cowboy life.

————. 2001. *In the days of the vaqueros.* New York: Clarion.

The conquistadores reintroduced the horse to the American continent in the early sixteenth century. The first cowboys were Spanish soldiers, settlers, and Native Americans in Mexico. Much of what we know of cowboy culture, including their clothing, tools, and language, evolved in this setting. This book supplements history texts and portrays cowboys as multi-dimensional historical figures. This book strongly supports the vocabulary activity in **Strategies to Teach Reading.**

Sandler, Martin W. 1994. *Cowboys: A Library of Congress book.* New York: Harper-Collins.

Suitable for elementary as well as older readers, Sandler's book combines simple text with a variety of illustrations, quotes, and song lyrics to paint a picture of the American cowboy. The book is organized into short sections on topics such as the open range, the roundup, the trail drive, cowboys, and outlaws. It provides a good source for short readings to be shared with the class around various cowboy topics.

Simmons, Marc. 2005. *Teddy's cattle drive: A story from history.* Albuquerque: University of New Mexico Press.

Noted New Mexico historian Marc Simmons has created a historically accurate and authentic look at a cattle drive based on the real-life experiences of E. C. "Teddy" Abbott along the Chisholm Trail in 1871. The illustrations of this picture story book help readers to visualize trail life.

Cowboys and Longhorns

A tongue of lightening splits the night sky. A boom of thunder follows. In an instant, 200 restless longhorns turn as a single animal and bolt across the scrubby plain. Each animal weighs close to a ton and sports sharp, pointed horns that may span a full eight feet. Each animal, in its desperate dash for freedom, will use its horns to slash and gore any creature in its way or to trample underfoot anyone unfortunate enough to fall down. Longhorns are strong, ferocious, independent, and determined. They are accustomed to roaming free and not at all interested in going anywhere they don't want to go. Trying to stop them is like trying to stop a speeding train. Yet, that is exactly the cowboy's job.

Stampedes were common on the long trail drives in which cowboys moved as many as 3,000 head of cattle at a time from the Texas ranches to the railway stations in Kansas and other northern states along the Chisholm or Goodnight Loving Trails. The cowboy's job was to control those cattle—to keep them moving in the right direction, to keep them together, and to keep them from stampeding. To do his job, the cowboy needed a number of skills. First and foremost, he needed to ride a horse well. Skill with a lariat came in handy. He probably needed to handle a gun so that he could shoot a threatening or charging steer—without hitting a horse or a fellow cowboy. Mostly, he needed to think like a longhorn, to be aware of conditions that might spook them, and to predict what they might do in various circumstances.

The cowboy's job was sometimes dangerous but, when things were going well, it was just plain boring. He rode for hours at a time. If he was a greenie (someone on his first drive), he rode drag at the back of the herd. A constant cloud of dust kicked up by 12,000 hooves stung the eyes and filled the mouth and dirtied the clothes. Biscuits, coffee, and beans were cooked and served around an open campfire. The cowboy then rolled himself in his blankets and slept on the ground until it was his turn to stand guard over the herd for the night. After the first few days, the cowboy was dirty, sleepless, tired, and perhaps lonely. The constant noise of 3,000 head of cattle made conversation almost impossible.

Movies, television, and books made popular an image of the cowboy as a handsome, slow-talking, horse-riding gun-slinger who fought for truth and justice and always won the heart of the prettiest girl in town. His enemies were the outlaws (often cowboys gone bad) who robbed banks and stagecoaches or Indians who attacked white settlers. The media cowboy was almost always an Anglo. Although bits and pieces of the image were based in reality, the total package was misleading.

The first cowboys were Mexican vaqueros and African Americans who had grown up as slaves on the Texas ranches prior to emancipation. These men were skillful, knowledgeable about cattle, and fearless. Later, young Anglo men seeking employment or adventure were hired on as greenies but often quit after one trail drive. There were also cowgirls, such as Annie Oakley and Calamity Jane, who were skilled riders, ropers, and shooters. Trail bosses, the men in charge, were almost always Anglo.

The days of the cowboy—open range, free-roaming longhorns, cow hunts, and long trail drives—lasted from about 1866 to 1895. It was fueled by the rise of the railroads, making transportation of the large herds possible, along with a growing taste for beef in the East. The gradual decline of the "wild" cattle, the rise of domesticated cattle farming, and the increase in packing plants closer to the point of sale decreased the need for the long cattle drives that were the backbone of the cowboy's livelihood. The hardworking cowboy and cowgirl, during their 20-year heyday, conquered a land and a wild animal and became an American icon of independence.

Song, "Git Along Little Dogies"

Text comes from Owen Wister, February 21, 1893. Mr. Wister was a writer of western fiction. His best known novel is *The Virginian.*

As I walked out one morning for pleasure, I met a cow puncher a jogging along: His hat was thrown back and his spurs was a-jingling along, And as he advanced he was singing this song:

"Sing hoop-li-o get along little dogies, for Wyoming shall be your new home. It's hooping and yelling and cursing those dogies to our misfortune but none of your own."

In the Springtime we round up the dogies, Slap on the brand and non off their tails: Then we cur her and her is inspected, And then we throw them on the trail.

"Sing hoop-li-o get along little dogies, for Wyoming shall be your new home. It's hooping and yelling and cursing those dogies to our misfortune but none of your own."

In the evening we round in the dogies, as they are grazing from herd all around. You have no idea the trouble they give us as we are holding them on the bedground.

"Sing hoop-li-o get along little dogies, for Wyoming shall be your new home. It's hooping and yelling and cursing those dogies to our misfortune but none of your own."

In the morning we throw off the bedground, Aiming to graze them an hour or two, When they are full, you think you can drive them on the trail, but damned if you do.

"Sing hoop-li-o get along little dogies, for Wyoming shall be your new home. It's hooping and yelling and cursing those dogies to our misfortune but none of your own."

Some fellows go on the trail for pleasure, but they have got this thing wrong: If it hadn't been for the troublesome dogies, I never would have thought about writing this song.

"Sing hoop-li-o get along little dogies, for Wyoming shall be your new home. It's hooping and yelling and cursing those dogies to our misfortune but none of your own."

Semantic Feature Analysis

Cowboys and Longhorns: Cowboy Language

Spanish Word	English Word	Definition	Minimal Change	Shortened Word	Corrupted Pronunciation	Different Word
1. *botas*						
2. *bronco*						
3. *chapparreras*						
4. *chaqueta*						
5. *espuelas*						
6. *lazo*						
7. *mesteño*						
8. *rancho*						
9. *la reata*						
10. *vaca*						
11. *vaquero*						

CHAPTER 9

The Orphan Trains

Chapter Preview

- **Gateway Books:** *Rodzina* by Karen Cushman; *Orphan Train Rider* by Andrea Warren
- **History Strategy:** Analyzing Illustrations
- **Reading Strategy:** I Poems
- **Historical Background:** Orphan Trains
- **Primary Source Document:** Book Illustrations
- **Graphic Organizer:** Historical Context Chart

Gateway Books

Cushman, Karen. 2003. *Rodzina.* New York: Random House.

Newbery Award–winning author Karen Cushman has created a fictional account of an orphan train rider in 1881. Big, tough, unpretty Rodzina is orphaned when her father is killed in an accident and her mother dies of wasting disease. She is plucked from life on the streets and sent to the Little Wanderers Refuge, where she is selected to join a group of orphans being taken by train to new homes and families in the West. The train makes a number of stops between Chicago and Utah. At each stop, the children are paraded in front of townspeople in the hope that someone will adopt them.

Rodzina narrates her own story, the events of the journey, and the tales of other orphans so that the experience takes on life and heart. The reader feels with Rodzina the pain of loss, the difficulties of the journey, and the ever present tension between the fear of not being chosen and the fear of being chosen by the wrong person. This book takes the reader into the mind and heart of an orphan as she struggles to make sense of the new world in which she finds herself. This fictional presentation balances the nonfiction of other featured and selected books and offers many opportunities for discussion about the orphan train experience.

This novel is a suitable read-aloud for upper elementary students and could be read independently by able readers in elementary and middle grade school.

Warren, Andrea. 1996. *Orphan train rider: One boy's true story.* New York: Scholastic.

While Cushman's book *Rodzina* is a fictional account of traveling the orphan train, Warren's book chronicles the actual journey of Lee Nailling. Through detailed descriptions and excerpts of interviews, Nailling remembers the events and circumstances of his life 75 years earlier. The reader experiences the death of a seven-year-old's mother, a father too distraught to take care of seven children, Lee's entry into an orphan asylum in New York, and finally, his cross-country journey on the orphan train. Lee explains the abrupt transition from one life to another with these words: "We went from being a close family to feeling like an outcast. Nobody visited, nobody wanted us, and nobody loved us. We were just two more homeless kids in a country that had too many."

Strategies to Teach History

Analyzing Illustrations

Building the social and cultural context of the time period is important for students to achieve historical understanding (see the **Windows into the Past** activity of chapter 2). In the 1890s, extreme poverty was common in New York City, and the combination of a large immigrant population and high unemployment propelled the city to a tipping point. Families were sometimes forced to make unfathomable decisions just to survive. Mothers had to abandon infants and young children were pushed from the home, living on the streets in dire poverty. To understand the desperation, students may listen at http://www.soundprint.org for biographical descriptions of the intense poverty that immigrant families faced in the late nineteenth and early twentieth centuries. This web-site contains primary documents, many of which are letters that were attached to children left on the doorsteps of family members or churches by forlorn parents unable to care for them any longer.

Charles Brace began the Children's Aid Society and the orphan train movement (see **Historical Background**) in the 1800s. The orphan trains carried children west, and their arrival in each town was advertised with handbills. People would meet the trains along the way looking for children to adopt. After a child or children were chosen, a 90-day trial period ensued. If all was acceptable, the children were indentured or adopted to the family.

Teaching Strategy

STEP 1

The teaching strategy is focused on helping students understand the place and time and the reasons the orphan trains were started. Reproduce copies of the illustrations from Charles Brace's book ***The Dangerous Classes of New York and Twenty Years' Work among Them*** (see the **Primary Source Document**). Ask students individually or in pairs to examine the series of illustrations and to formulate a list of questions about the images. The purpose for developing the questions is to place the students in an inquiry-based—rather than a descriptive—mode. After a suitable work period, reconvene the students as a whole group and list the questions generated in a central place for reference.

STEP 2

Organize students into small groups to research what was happening during the 1880s and 1890s in the larger cities of the United States, especially New York. Provide each group with the **Graphic Organizer** for this chapter. The **Graphic Organizer** is designed to look at the social climate from a variety of viewpoints, including economic, cultural, and governance stances. Through this assignment, the students can discover for themselves the social conditions that led to the orphan trains.

STEP 3

On completion of the **Graphic Organizer,** students share what they have learned in a class discussion. Trends for the teacher to highlight as students share are the influx of immigrants and the extreme poverty, unemployment, and over-population of New York City.

STEP 4

Students revisit the illustrations as the teacher provides the labels for each: "the homeless waif," "the young thief," "the drunkard," and "the prisoner." This transforms the illustrations from a tragic story to a public warning about what can happen if someone does not intervene in the lives of homeless children. Charles Loring Brace began the Children's Aid Society and the orphan trains as an answer to the problem.

STEP 5

Provide students with the following quote from Charles Loring Brace and connect his solution with the orphan trains:

The United States have the enormous advantage over all other countries, in the treatment of difficult questions of pauperism and reform, that they possess a practically unlimited area of arable land. The demand for labor on this land is beyond any present supply. Moreover, the cultivators of the soil are in America our most solid and intelligent class. From the nature of their circumstances, their laborers, or "help," must be members of their families and share in their social tone. It is, accordingly, of the utmost importance to them to train up children who shall aid in their work, and be associates of their own children. A servant who is nothing but a servant would be, with them, disagreeable and inconvenient. They like to educate their own "help." With their overflowing supply of food also, each new mouth in the household brings no drain on their means. Children are a blessing, and the mere feeding of a young boy or girl is not considered at all.

After reading the quote, ask students to do a quick write using the quote, the **Primary Source Document,** and information gained from their research and the completion of the **Graphic Organizer.** The quick write should address what they now understand about Charles Loring Brace and the reasons behind the creation of the orphan trains.

Depending on the time constraints of the classroom, have students discuss the effectiveness of the orphan trains.

Extension

Photos of orphan train riders can be accessed through the web-site of the Children's Aid Society (http://www.childrensaidsociety.org) or the Library of Congress (http://www.loc.gov). Providing visual images to students helps them to connect with the experience. Ask students to research and look for images on these two sites or the teacher may request copies of images from the different organizations for students to see the real faces of the orphan train riders.

Strategies to Teach Reading

I Poems

One of the goals of critical reading is being able to understand and restate another's point of view. This is a skill that can be applied in both fiction and nonfiction. Creating an I poem requires careful attention in reading and the necessity of making inferences based on the information provided—both skills that student readers need to develop.

Like the **Found Poetry** of chapter 1, these poem frames engage students in summarizing textual information and identifying important ideas. At the same time, the strategy encourages imagination and empathy as students think through that information from the point of view and emotional context of the character. Writing is scaffolded by the frame so that it is not burdensome, even for struggling students.

I poems, which are discussed by Tompkins and McGee (1993), scaffold student writing and thinking. At its most basic, the structure calls for students to create an unrhymed poem with each line beginning with "I," forcing them to consider the chosen character's point of view. Depending on the class of students and the goals of the activity, we sometimes structure the activity further with sentence frames such as those shown in the following teaching activity.

Teaching Activity

An initial experience with this process might be done whole-class as the teacher solicits ideas and models the actual writing for students. The teacher will preselect a text to form the basis of the activity. Preparation is minimal, perhaps consisting of an overhead or large chart listing the poem frame.

The choice of sentence stems focuses student attention on various aspects of the character's experience. Stems such as "I see," "I hear," and "I touch" focus on sensory experience; "I do" and "I try" highlight physical actions; "I think," "I wonder," and "I say" delve into the thinking and reasoning of the character; and "I worry," "I fear," "I celebrate," and "I love" lead students to consider the character's emotional life. The I poem frame focuses on a single character such as Rodzina in the featured novel (fiction) or Lee Nailling in the nonfiction selection. Completion of the I poem is an effective character study. Repetition of the "I am" stem at the beginning and end of the poem brings the thoughts together and provides closure. Possible sentence stems for an "I am" poem follow:

I Am Poem

I am
I wonder
I see

I hear
I want
I pretend
I say
I worry
I try
I hope
I am

Student Activity

After a whole-class experience in which the process is explained and modeled, students can easily complete this activity as independent work following a reading selection. The frame may be developed by the teacher and posted or copied for students to use. Students with more experience can create their own frames within guidelines set by the teacher.

The "We Are" poem frame can be substituted for the "I AM" frame to encourage students to think about a group of people such as the orphan train riders. Following is an example of a "We Are" frame. Using this after reading the **Historical Background** for this chapter or at the end of the unit of study allows students to summarize what they have learned as well as connect to the feelings and emotions surrounding historical figures and events:

We Are Poem

We are
We wonder
We hear
We see
We feel
We worry
We understand
We say
We dream
We try
We are

Typically the "We are" stem at the beginning and end of the poem identifies the topic. In this case, this stem would read, "We are orphan train riders."

Extension

We suggest "I Am" and "We Are" poems as foundational activities for developing poems for two or more voices, a strategy which is discussed in chapter 10.

Unit Timeline

- Begin this unit with the study of Charles Loring Brace and the orphan trains, as described in **Strategies to Teach History.** Supplementing this activity with pictures of actual people who rode the orphan trains, as suggested in the extension, will help students to connect emotionally with people whose lives are being studied.

- Read the **Historical Background** as shared (see chapter 4) or independent reading.
- Engage students with one or both of the featured selections, which balance fiction and nonfiction accounts of the orphan trains. These may be offered to students through whole-class read-alouds, novel study, or excerpts.
- Have students write I poems about a chosen character, either fiction or nonfiction. The character could be selected from one of the featured selections or may be someone students have encountered in their research.
- "We Are" poems can become an effective summary activity for the unit. Teachers might elect to have students write "We are orphan train riders" instead of or in addition to the I poem suggested in the preceding step.

Adult Bibliography

Holt, Marilyn. 1994. *The orphan trains: Placing out in America.* Omaha: University of Nebraska Press.

Describing the resettlement of at least 200,000 children during the years 1850–1930, Holt critically examines the successes and failures of the orphan train experiment. Through the use of oral histories, institutional records, and newspaper accounts, the orphan train experience comes alive for the reader.

O'Conner, Stephen. 2001. *Orphan trains: The story of Charles Loring Brace and the children he saved and failed.* New York: Houghton Mifflin.

A critical view of the philosophy of the man who began the orphan trains and his motivation behind the experiment.

Student Bibliography

Bunting, Eve. 2000. *Train to somewhere.* New York: Clarion Books.

This book will be too young for some classes. We recommend it, however, because of the poignant story that deeply engages the reader in the fears and joys of a group of orphan train riders.

Warren, Andrea. 2001. *We rode the orphan trains.* New York: Houghton Mifflin.
This book chronicles eight orphan train riders and their experiences. The stories stretch between 1854 and 1929. Included tales range from the horrors of abuse to the fulfillment of a dream of becoming a family.

Orphan Trains

Trains traveled east. Trains traveled west. To many people, train travel was an adventure, a business plan, a scenic journey. To some people, however, the trains represented loss and opportunity.

In the late 1800s, trains were bringing Native American children from their homes and families in Indian territory to the Indian boarding schools. At much the same time, other groups of children were leaving life on the streets of the big eastern cities to find families on the farms and in the small towns of rural America.

This was the period of the American Industrial Revolution. The growing factories provided job opportunities for many Americans and for the growing immigrant population. Unfortunately, life in the city and in the factories was hard. Wages were low. Families crowded into small, squalid tenements. Illness and accidents were common. Many children lost one or both parents; others were in families that simply could not support them. As a consequence, many children were forced onto the streets to sell matches and newspapers, to beg and steal to eat, and to find shelter as they could. These homeless youngsters (both male and female) often formed gangs for protection and survival. Sometimes the gangs engaged in criminal activities. They were "street rats" or "street urchins."

In 1853 a young minister named Charles Loring Brace was so moved by the plight of homeless children that he decided to do something about it. He founded the Children's Aid Society of New York. Recognizing that orphanages could not hold the immense number of children who were abandoned or orphaned, Brace conceived the idea of sending them west. His belief was that farm families of the Midwest would have room at their tables and in their hearts for another child. In return for help with the tasks of daily living, children would be fed, clothed, loved, and given a better life.

Starting in 1854, trains left New York City with groups of orphans accompanied by two adult agents. The children ranged from infants to teenagers. Some were actual orphans; some had been taken from neglectful or abusive families. Still others had been given to the orphanages by families that could not care for them. Notices were posted ahead of the trains, announcing the date and time of arrival. Families from the local communities were invited to meet the children and choose one. When the train actually arrived, children were cleaned up and displayed (on a stage of sorts) to waiting families. Children were warned to be on their best behavior so that they would be chosen.

The intentions were good; the results were mixed. Some children did indeed find loving homes and a much improved life. Others were chosen by individuals or families looking for cheap labor. While some children were loved and cherished, others were treated as slaves. Some children grew to adulthood in happy homes; others ran away or died.

Even for children who were well placed, the experience was difficult at times. Almost all described the process of being paraded for inspection as traumatic, fearing rejection if you were not chosen, but also fearing the unknown if you were. Older children remembered and missed families they had lost or left behind and suffered the pain of being separated from brothers and sisters who were adopted by different families.

In the years between 1854 and 1929, an estimated 150,000 to 400,000 children and young people rode the orphan trains west. Some are still alive today.

Book Illustrations

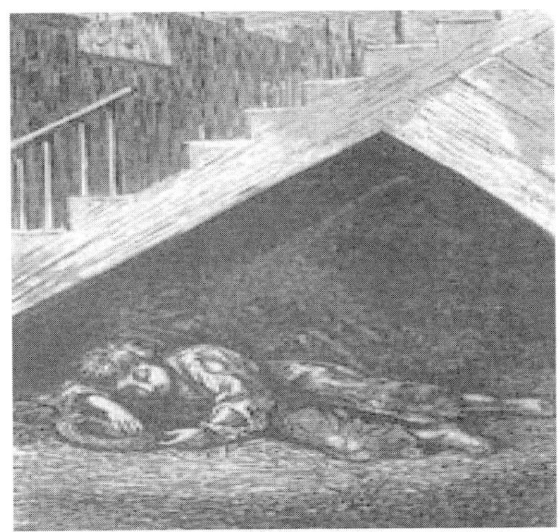

Source: Charles Loring Brace, *The Dangerous Classes of New York and Twenty Years' Work Among Them* (New York: Wynkoop and Hallenbeck, 1872), i–ii, 225–227, 234–235.

From *Gateways to Westward Expansion: Using Literature and Primary Sources to Enhance Reading Instruction and Historical Understanding* by Ann Claunch and Linda L. Tripp. Westport, CT: Teacher Ideas Press. Copyright © 2009.

Building Historical Context

Teacher: Guiding Questions, Who, What, When, Why, How?

To understand the orphan trains, it is important for students to research the time and place of the late nineteenth century. Provide small groups of students with a collection of resources like the three below so students can gather information for discussion of the world of the orphan trains.

1. http://kclibrary.lonestar.edu/19thcentury1860.htm
2. Grun, Bernard. 2005. *The timetables of history: A horizontal linkage of people and events.* New York: Touchstone Press.
3. Urdang, Laurence. 2001. *The timetables of American history.* New York: Touchstone Press.

Political	Intellectual	Cultural	Social	Economics	Technological
What was happening in the national government? What laws were being passed?	What social movements were being initiated?	What books were being written? What art was popular? What were people doing for entertainment?	What was the population of the United States? Were people in urban areas, or were they working in rural areas? Two web-sites that help include the following: http://fisher.lib.virginia.edu/collections/stats/histcensus/ http://www.census.gov/population/www/censusdata/hiscendata.html	How people provided for their needs. What goods were being exported? Imported?	What inventions were new?

CHAPTER 10

The Women of the Westward Movement

Chapter Preview

- **Gateway Books:** *Into a New Country* by Liza Ketchem; *Black Women of the Old West* by William Katz
- **History Strategy:** Source Boxes
- **Reading Strategy:** Poems for Two Voices
- **Historical Background:** Women of the Westward Movement
- **Primary Source Document:** A Letter from Mrs. Tape
- **Graphic Organizer:** Shared Experiences

Gateway Books

Ketchem, Liza. 2001. *Into a new country: Eight remarkable women of the West.* Boston: Little, Brown.

When my daughter was eight, she came home with this question: "Why are all the heroines in history men?" Besides the obvious gender confusion of heroes and heroines, as a third grader, she had determined that women had no place in her history books. This is still a challenge in the teaching of American history. Traditional history establishes a single gender as the significant contributor to the settling of the West, while remaining silent about women. Women are mentioned in secondary roles as helpers. Seldom are they illuminated as rich contributors to the events of the nineteenth century.

Books like *Into a New Country: Eight Remarkable Women of the West* present an important piece of the history that is often forgotten or ignored. Liza Ketchem presents a panoramic view of women who came west. The eight stories are diverse and represent not only the hardships that the women suffered, but also how each thrived and became an important part of the economic and social tapestry.

Ketchem has carefully researched and brought the individual woman into focus. The reader is captivated by stories of confrontation, hardship, perseverance, and determination. My daughter would be proud.

Katz, William. 1995. *Black women of the old West.* New York: Antheneum Press.

Women of color find that history has further ignored their contributions. Although they were in the minority as numbers of Americans moved west, African American women made a significant impact. They ran laundries, drove stagecoaches, fought for integrated schools, and became civil rights leaders, while being devoted mothers, wives, and friends.

Luticia Parsons was a nurse to the buffalo soldiers in the Southwest. Martha Williams helped care for orphans in Arizona and New Mexico, while her mother, Cathay Williams, served secretly as a buffalo soldier by disguising herself as a man. These are a few of the stories told in ***Black Women of the West.***

These stories provide the reader with a deeper understanding of the profound legacy that began as our nation grew and of those who took risks for a new and better life. Katz's book is important for its fresh perspective on the westward movement and for the presentation of diverse people who played a role in the settlement of the West.

Strategies to Teach History

Source Boxes

Source boxes are created by the students with the purpose of studying different historical personages through artifacts. Images of the person and her family, written documents, both personal and official, and other sources construct a mental image of the person's life and her contribution to history.

Students choose a person to research related to the classroom curriculum and then access different archives on the Internet and visit school and public libraries to gather information on the person selected. The student is taking the part of a "history detective," putting pieces of information together to construct a complex understanding of the historical person and the time in which she lived.

Teaching Activity

This activity is designed to highlight the women who had a significant part in the settlement of the West. Individually or in pairs, students select a "woman of the West" from the following list and research the individual, with the purpose of creating a source box of the woman's life to present to the class in two weeks' time. The source box (a shoe box or covered cereal box) is a collection of artifacts. The artifacts placed inside the box are meant to illustrate and give information about the woman's life and her contribution to history.

The names appearing in the following list are those mentioned in the **Gateway Books** for this chapter. The list can be expanded by further research and by suggestions from the students:

Katherine Ryan	**Mary Fields**
Biddy Mason	**Mary Pleasant**
Lotta Crabtree	**Lulu Sadler Craig**
Lucy Parsons	**Elvira Conley**
Susette and Susan LaFlesche	**Clara Brown**
Mary McGladery Tape	

The source box should contain a minimum of 10 items. The contents should include, but are not limited to, the following:

- An image of the woman you are researching; images of relatives or friends
- A two-page biography of the woman (where she was born, her early life, and her marital status, children, and contributions to history)
- A **Primary Source Document** relating to your woman (contracts, a policy she influenced, a copy of a journal or diary)
- Examples of art, literature, fashion, architecture, tools, or technology common to her era and her region

The **Primary Source Document** for this chapter is a letter Mary McGladery Tape wrote fighting against discrimination in 1885. This is an example of an artifact that might be placed in a source box for Mary Tape. Distribute copies of the letter and ask students to read silently as the teacher reads aloud. Students must consider the following:

- What is the date of the letter? Where is the letter mailed, to and from?
- What do we know about this time period?
- What is the tone of the letter? What is the evidence supporting this assumption?
- What is the purpose of the letter?
- What does the letter tell us about the author? Cite specific wording as evidence for your assumptions.
- Was the letter successful? How can we find out?

The process teaches students how to mine a document for information about a particular individual. In this way, we build a picture of individual women who lived in the West and how their voices and actions influenced history.

Sharing

After a period of research, students may share their source boxes with the class in small groups. Organize students into groups of four. Each group should have researched four different women. Distribute a **Graphic Organizer** to each group. The **Graphic Organizer** for this chapter is meant to be used in the small groups. In the four overlapping quadrants, students record what is distinctive about each woman's choices and actions. In the middle space, students record experiences that the women shared. The purpose of the four quadrants is to engage students in sharing their research and lead them to identify similarities in challenges faced by women on the frontier in the late nineteenth century.

Strategies to Teach Reading

Poems for Two Voices

The I poems and We poems discussed in chapter 9 offer students the opportunity to summarize information and to think through the perspective of a historical character, fictional or real. Composing a poem for two voices builds on those skills, asking students to further develop their thinking by comparing and contrasting the perspectives of varying viewpoints.

In 1988 Paul Fleischman published *Joyful Noise: Poems for Two Voices.* The book went on to win the Newbery Medal for literature. In this book, Fleischman offers a number of poems about insects. Each poem involves at least two speakers (or groups of speakers), who speak both antiphonally and chorally. The poem is arranged on the page in two columns, showing where speakers alternate and where they speak together.

After the book appeared, teachers began to adapt the process for student writing. It is particularly relevant to social studies because the process of creating the poem requires students to consider different points of view with an eye to finding both commonalities and conflict between them. Using the poem for two voices format can lead students to compare and contrast historical figures from the same era, fictional and nonfictional (even nonhuman) characters, and historical personages of differing eras and time periods. Imagine, for example, conversations between the cowboy and the longhorn, an orphan train rider and an Indian boarding school student, or a railroad rider and a coolie worker. Using the poem for two voices strategy offers a scaffolded experience for students in contrasting the viewpoints of different characters in a personal way.

Preparation

To be most effective, teachers will need to invest a small amount of time in building models for students. The first step is simply to expose them to a variety of poems for two voices over a period of time. Reproduce a copy of a poem and spend a few minutes at the beginning of the class period having students read the poem chorally. Doing this every day for several days and introducing a variety of two-voice poems builds a strong model for students. Fleischman's book offers several selections. "The Honeybees" is particularly relevant in showing differing opinions.

Teaching Activity

Once students have had several experiences with the poems, introduce the writing activity. The teacher may engage students in a whole-class activity before assigning this as independent work. Pair students and give them the following guidelines:

- Select two characters. (The teacher may provide a preselected list from which students choose in this initial phase or may assign every partnership the same two characters.)
- Discuss the first character and write an I poem about him/her. (This step presupposes that students have read and digested information about the individuals selected. If not, the teacher may need to assign reading or research.)
- Discuss the second character and write an I poem about him/her.
- Develop a Venn diagram comparing and contrasting the two individuals or refer to the "Shared Experiences" **Graphic Organizer** completed in **Strategies to Teach History.**
- Fold a paper in thirds. Assign the left-hand column to one individual and the right-hand column to the other. Write statements and short phrases that these individuals might speak. Use the center column to write statements and short phrases that they might say together. Use your I poems and your Venn diagram to help you.
- Rewrite the poem in the modeled poem for two voices style.

Sharing

Plan a time period for student partnerships to share their writing by reading the poems orally. Poems can also be shared by posting them around the classroom. After everyone has shared, ask students to discuss what they learned from the activity.

Poem for Two Voices is an excellent collaborative or cooperative learning activity as it engages students in face-to-face discussion. They must depend on one another to complete the project.

This activity is an excellent way to summarize a small unit of study such as "women of the westward movement." The strategy can also serve to summarize and bring conclusion to a much larger unit of study by assigning individuals from different time periods (e.g., a buffalo soldier and a coolie) and having students compare experiences and perspectives across time.

Unit Timeline

- Engage students with one or both of the featured selections, which offer accounts of the women of the West. These may be presented to students through whole-class read-alouds of excerpts or a chapter per day. The **Historical Background** for this chapter also briefly summarizes information about a variety of women. This may be a shared (chapter 4) or independent reading.
- After the introduction of a number of different women, have students select a woman to be researched and begin working on the **Source Boxes** described in **Strategies to Teach History.**
- Students share information about individual women gleaned from their research. Follow the directions outlined in **Strategies to Teach Reading** to compare and contrast different women in a **Poem for Two Voices.**

Adult Bibliography

Luchetti, Cathy, and Carol Olwell. 2001. *Women of the West.* New York: W. C. Norton.

Voices and images build the vision of daily life on the frontier for minority women. This book fills in many of the omitted voices in American history.

Peavy, Linda, and Ursula Smith. 1998. *Pioneer women: The lives of women on the frontier.* Oklahoma City: University of Oklahoma Press.

The black-and-white photographs capture the hardships of an unforgiving terrain. The authors reveal, in the words of the women, the difficulties of facing each day, from the mundane tasks of securing clean drinking water to the fears of isolation and the unknown and the hopelessness of losing children to disease and accidents.

Student Bibliography

Bentley, Judith. 1995. *Brides/midwives and widows.* New York: Twenty-first Century Books.

This book describes various ways that groups of women came to the West: with husbands, seeking husbands (mail-order brides), as prostitutes or slaves, and as widows carrying on after a husband's death. The narrative includes brief information on a few individuals who left records.

Fox, Mary V. 1991. ***The story of the women who shaped the West.*** Chicago: University of Chicago Press.

For a slightly less seasoned reader, this book, with large print and a variety of images, supports students in understanding the vital role women played in the westward movement.

Freedman, Russell. 2001. ***Children of the wild West.*** New York: Houghton Mifflin.

Through images and text, Freedman depicts another forgotten group involved in settling the frontier: children.

Wooldridge, Connie N., and Jacqueline Rogers. 2001. ***When Esther Morris headed west: Women, Wyoming, and the right to vote.*** New York: Holiday House.

This humorous picture book, suitable for all ages, looks at the life of a woman who not only embraced the idea of women's suffrage, but lived it, becoming a voter and the first female justice of the peace. Wyoming Territory was the first part of the United States to give women the right to vote, in 1869.

Women of the Westward Movement

In the 1800s, women had few choices when it came to life roles. Most were wives and mothers who worked long hours to grow, preserve, and prepare food, to clothe their families, and to maintain the home. Women whose husbands or fathers were wealthy led a more privileged life in terms of ease and comfort, but they were also expected to make the home the center of their existence. Men held the money and the power in all aspects of life, and women were ruled by men. There were exceptions, however: strong, determined, intelligent women of all races and walks of life who defied the social order of the day.

Bridget Mason, known as "Biddy," traveled west as the slave of a Mormon family emigrating to Utah in 1848. She walked the entire way at the back of the wagon train, eating dust, caring for her three small children, and aiding anyone who might need her nursing skills. Three years later, Biddy's owner moved again, taking Biddy and her family along. Their destination was California. They discovered after arriving that slavery was illegal there. Fearing the loss of his slaves, Biddy's owner decided to move again to Texas. Biddy recognized an opportunity and, with help from friends, petitioned the court for her freedom. It was an act of extreme courage since losing could mean a severe beating and a continued life of slavery. The judge ruled in her favor. Although Biddy never learned to read or write, she became a free woman of property and wealth, who generously helped anyone in her community who was in need.

Susette and Susan LaFlesche were sisters and daughters of an Omaha chief, who raised them with knowledge and respect for their cultural traditions. He also encouraged them to become educated in the schools run by whites. Both young women eventually traveled east, where they received a higher education. Susette, also known as Bright Eyes, became a teacher and later traveled the country, speaking on behalf of her people and against the injustices done to them. Susan, 11 years younger, finished medical school (an outstanding accomplishment for any woman in that time period) and returned home to provide medical care and education to the people of the reservation.

Mary McGladery was a Chinese orphan (given a Scottish name by Presbyterian missionaries in China) who immigrated to Gum Saan (the Mountain of Gold, the Chinese name for California) in 1868. There she continued her education in a missionary school and eventually married Joseph Tape and raised four children. When her children were excluded from public school because they were Chinese, Mary wrote letters, went to court, and campaigned endlessly for equal educational opportunities for all. She was a painter, an innovative photographer, and extremely proficient in the technology (telephone, telegraph) that was in its infancy during her lifetime.

During the Yukon gold rush, a 28-year-old nurse named Kate Ryan traveled alone to Alaska and mushed her way (she had never handled a dog sled before) to the interior. In the following years, she ran a restaurant, took in laundry, nursed the sick, made and lost a fortune, and became the first female Canadian Mountie.

These women, along with others, such as Bethenia Owens-Adair, Lotta Crabtree, Annie Oakley, and Esther Morris, pushed the limits of women's roles during their lifetimes.

From *Gateways to Westward Expansion: Using Literature and Primary Sources to Enhance Reading Instruction and Historical Understanding* by Ann Claunch and Linda L. Tripp. Westport, CT: Teacher Ideas Press. Copyright © 2009.

Some of their accomplishments, such as acting on stage, speaking in public, becoming doctors, or seeking justice in the court system, would seem commonplace in the cultural environment of today. However, in the nineteenth century, these accomplishments were born of struggle, perseverance, and the ability to look beyond the expectations of family and society to consider new possibilities.

A Letter from Mrs. Tape

1769 Green Street,
San Francisco, April 8, 1885.

To the Board of Education—dear sirs: I see that you are going to make all sorts of excuses to keep my child out off the Public schools. Dear sirs, Will you please to tell me! Is it a disgrace to be Born a Chinese? Didn't God make us all!!! What right have you to bar my children out of the school because she is a chinese decend. They is no other worldly reason that you could keep her out, except that. I suppose, you all goes to churches on Sundays! Do you call that a Christian act to compell my little children to go so far to a school that is made in purpose for them. My children don't dress like the other Chinese. They look just as phunny amongst them as the Chinese dress in Chinese look amongst you Caucasians. Besides, if I had any wish to send them to a chinese school I could have sent them two years ago without going to all this trouble. You have expended a lot of the Public money foolishly, all because of a one poor little Child. Her playmates is all Caucasians ever since she could toddle around. If she is good enough to play with them! Then is she not good enough to be in the same room and studie with them? You had better come and see for yourselves. See if the Tape's is not same as other Caucasians, except in features. It seems no matter how a Chinese may live and dress so long as you know they Chinese. Then they are hated as one. . .

Source: Alta, April 16, 1885.

Women of the West

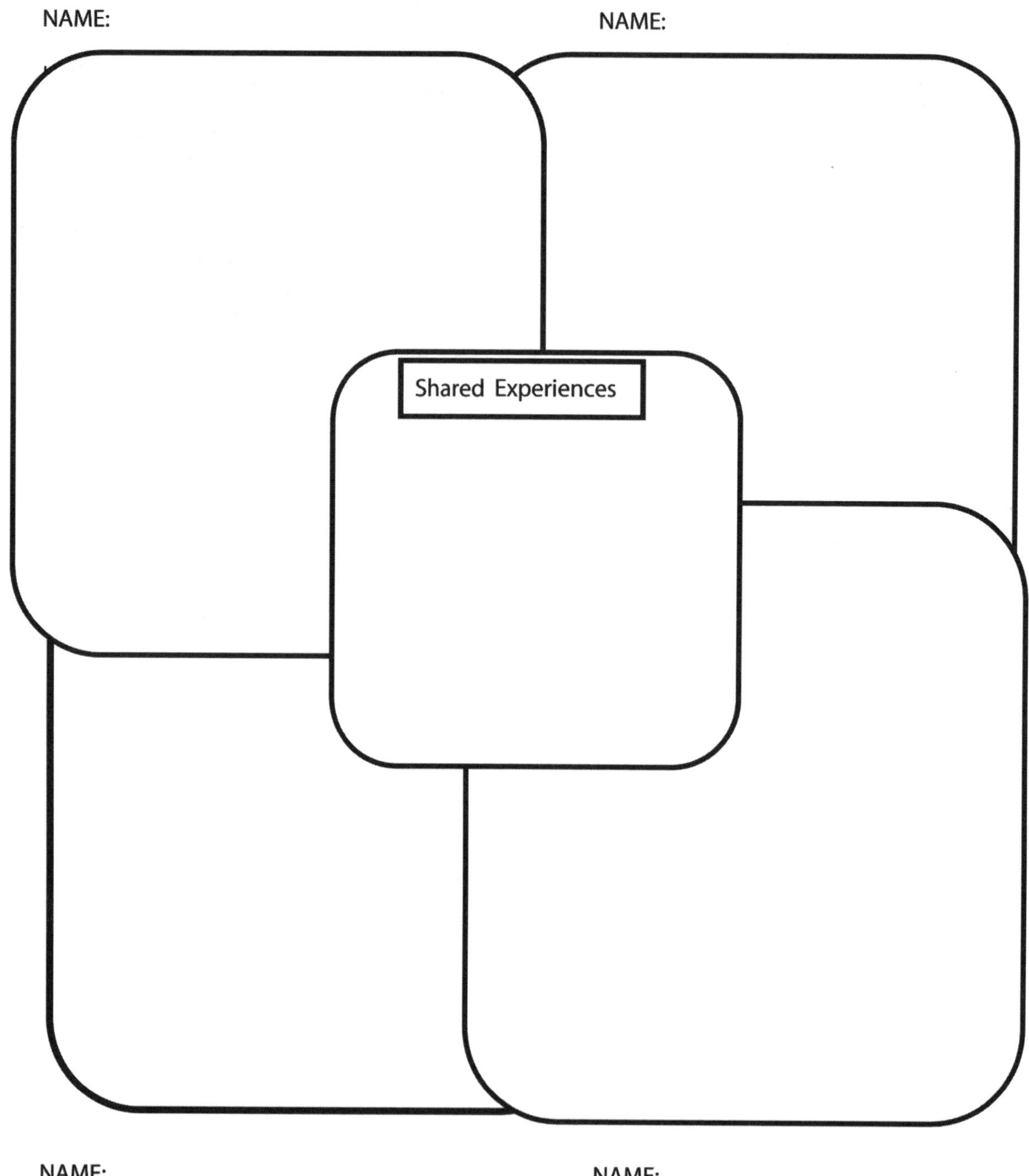

Assessment

Listed below are a number of activities from the chapters of this book that provide opportunities for performance assessment. Most are multi-layered. Teachers are encouraged to use the rubric in Appendix B as a beginning point and to specify requirements for a particular task.

Analyzing Correspondence (chapter 6)
Analyzing Photographs (chapter 7)
Analyzing Quotes (chapter 7)
Cartoon Analysis (chapter 5)
Found Poetry (chapter 1)
I Poems (chapter 9)
Poems for Two Voices (chapter 10)
Song Analysis (chapter 8)
Source Boxes (chapter 10)
Studying the Individual in History (chapter 4)
Using Primary Source Documents (chapter 1)
Weighing the Evidence (chapter 3)
Windows into the Past (chapter 2)

Preliminary Assessment Rubric

Preliminary Assessment Rubric

Criteria	Exceeds	Masters	Needs Improvement	Beginning Steps
Addresses all listed aspects of the task	100%	85%	70%	Less than 50%
Analysis shows evidence of historical understanding	Displays original thought and provides solid evidence for thinking; represents multiple points of view	Shows logical reasoning and provides solid evidence	Incomplete or illogical conclusions or no evidence for thinking	Lacks conclusion or supporting evidence
Information is complete and accurate	Supports information with multiple source citations	Supports important information with source citations	Some information is inaccurate; information is unsupported by sources	Much information is inaccurate or unsupported
Presentation (oral or written) shows attention to detail: spelling, organization, and so on	Presentation is well organized, contains no errors; visuals are present	Presentation is organized and contains minimal errors	Presentation lacks necessary organization to be clear to reader/listener; visuals do not clarify	Presentation is unclear, messy, does not communicate to audience

References

Allen, Janet. 2002. *On the same page: Shared reading beyond the primary grades.* New York: Stenhouse.

Allen, Janet, and Christine Landaker. 2005. *Reading history: A practical guide to improving literacy.* New York: Oxford University Press.

Beck, Isabel L., Margaret G. McKeown, and Linda Kucan. 2002. *Bringing words to life: Robust vocabulary instruction.* New York: Guilford Press.

Brophy, Jere, and Janet Alleman. 2005. *Children's thinking about cultural universals.* Philadelphia, PA: Erlbaum Associates.

Claunch, Ann. 2002. How Nine- and Ten-year Olds Construct Historical Thinking by Reading Children's Literature. PhD diss., University of New Mexico.

Holdaway, Don. 1980. *Independence in reading: A handbook on individualized procedures.* Gosford, NSW, Aust.: Ashton Scholastic.

Kuhn, Melaine. 2005. Presentation at International Reading Association Conference. San Antonio, TX.

Marzano, Robert J., Debra Pickering, and Jane E. Pollock. 2001. *Classroom instruction that works: Research-based strategies for increasing student achievement.* Alexandria, VA: ASCD.

Tompkins, Gail E., and Lea M. McGee. 1993. *Teaching reading with literature: Case studies to action plans.* New York: Macmillan.

Vygotsky, Lev. 1962. *Thought and language.* Cambridge, MA: MIT Press.

Web-sites

Center for the Study of Historical Consciousness, University of British Columbia: http://www.cshc.ubc.ca/

Gilder Lehrman: http://www.gilderlehrman.org/

History Channel: http://www.history.com/media.do

Library of Congress: http://www.loc.gov/

National Archives: http://www.archives.gov/

National History Day: http://www.nhd.org/

Our Documents: http://www.ourdocuments.gov/

Index

About the Authors

As veteran teachers of students K–12 and adult educators at the University of New Mexico and Albuquerque Public Schools, the authors bring practical and theoretical expertise to the book.

ANN CLAUNCH, PhD, is currently the director of curriculum for National History Day and is a professor emeritus from the University of New Mexico. As a veteran teacher and teacher educator, she now writes history curricula and presents nationally on teaching methods for history education.

LINDA L. TRIPP was a classroom teacher for more than 30 years, teaching a range of ages, subjects, and grades. She also worked as an adjunct instructor in University of New Mexico teacher education programs and as an instructional coach, supporting students in developing historical understanding and facilitating teachers in improving instruction.